parallax

SUBSCRIPTION INFORMATION

parallax is a peer-reviewed journal, published quarterly, by Routledge Journals, an imprint of Taylor & Francis Ltd, 4 Park Square, Milton Park, Abingdon, Oxon OX14 4RN, UK.

Annual Subscription, Volume 10, 2004 (Print ISSN 1353-4645)

Institutional	$365.00	£221.00
Individual	$90.00	£55.00

An institutional subscription to the print edition includes free access for any number of concurrent users across a local area network to the online edition, ISSN 1460-700X.

For more information, visit our website: http://www.tandf.co.uk/journals

For a complete and up-to-date guide to Taylor & Francis Group's journals and books publishing programmes, and details on advertising in our journals, visit our website: http://www.tandf.co.uk/journals

Dollar rates apply to subscribers in all countries except the UK and the Republic of Ireland where the pound sterling price applies. All subscriptions are payable in advance and all rates include postage. Journals are sent by air to the USA, Canada, Mexico, India, Japan and Australasia. Subscriptions are entered on an annual basis, i.e. January to December. Payment may be made by sterling cheque, dollar cheque, international money order, National Giro, or credit card (AMEX, VISA, Mastercard).

Ordering information:
USA/Canada: Routledge Journals, Taylor & Francis Inc., Journals Department, 325 Chestnut Street, 8th Floor, Philadelphia, PA 19106, USA. **UK/Europe/Rest of World:** Routledge Journals, Taylor & Francis Ltd, Rankine Road, Basingstoke, Hampshire RG24 8PR, UK.

Advertising enquiries to:
USA/Canada: The Advertising Manager, Taylor & Francis Inc., 325 Chestnut Street, 8th Floor, Philadelphia, PA 19106, USA. Tel: +1 (215) 625 8900; Fax: +1 (215) 625 2240. **EU/RoW:** The Advertising Manager, Taylor & Francis Ltd, 4 Park Square, Milton Park, Abingdon, Oxon OX14 4RN, UK. Tel: +44 (0)1235 828600; Fax: +44 (0)1235 829000.

The print edition of this journal is typeset, printed and bound by the Charlesworth Group, Huddersfield, UK on ANSI conforming acid free paper. The online edition of this journal is hosted by MetaPress at http://www.journalsonline.tandf.co.uk.

parallax (USPS permit number 021 375) is published quarterly (in January–March, April–June, July–September and October–December). The 2003 US institutional subscription price is $365.00. Periodicals postage paid at Champlain, NY, by US Mail Agent IMS of New York, 100 Walnut Street, Champlain, NY.

US Postmaster: Please send address changes to TPAR, PO Box 1518, Champlain, NY 12919, USA.

parallax

Issue 31 April–June 2004

auditing culture

parallax

visceral reason

The July 2005 issue of **parallax** will be devoted to the topic of 'visceral reason' as a figure for the self-preservative logic at stake in the resurgence of adrenally charged leftovers from histories of persecution. This term is intended to prompt reflection on the relationship between such histories and the affective detritus they leave behind in the form of *ressentiment*, paranoia, anxiety, despair, melancholy, learned helplessness, resistance or, perhaps, forgiveness. The special editor seeks papers that conceptualize these moods in the context of interdisciplinary theories of culture and society. The ultimate aim is to consider the relevance of these concepts for cultural critique and for understanding recent events.

Please send completed articles of approximately 4500–5000 words by August 5th, 2004 to the special editor:

Karyn Ball, Assistant Professor
Department of English
University of Alberta
3-5 Humanities Centre
Edmonton, AB T6G 2E5
Canada
Fax: (780) 492-8142
Email: Karyn.ball@ualberta.ca

call for papers

parallax, 2004, vol. 10, no. 2, 1–2

Editorial Sounding: Auditing Culture

*Writing is a duty, suggests Lyotard, not the right – birthright, right
of anointment, or usurped right – of the intellectuals. The duty to
express what otherwise would remain silent [...] The assumption of
such a duty means moving in the dark, taking risks – taking
responsibility for the audibility of the numb.*
Zygmunt Bauman, *Life in Fragments*, 241–242

This issue of **parallax** owes its initial impetus to a resolutely singular moment: the
R.A.E.[1] fuelled closure of the former *Centre for Contemporary Cultural Studies* at
Birmingham University – an institution of singular importance for Cultural Studies'
own founding myth.[2] However, if this closure is 'exemplary' – with all the irony
we can muster in that phrase – it is not exemplary of the status of Cultural Studies
per se, but rather of the deleterious effects of a certain 'coercive accountability'[3] of
Academy to State to Market in Britain; i.e. the unchecked migration of 'auditing'
procedures/discourses and rationalized performance criteria from corporate (*deemed*
'private') to academic (*deemed* 'public') institutions, under the mediating administration
of the State. This migration has taken the form of an authoritarian 'calling to
account': a command that the subject/institution render itself audi(ta)ble and
(ac)countable to the ears of the State via the Market, or the Market via the State; a
tautological demand for an audience with 'excellence'[4] – 'excellence' is that which is
'excellent'! – issued and overwhelmingly met with private dissent and public silence; or
with the spurious and often competitive deployment of cultural capital, in the shape of
different theoretical lexicons, or economic capital, in the name of a national funding
war.

Nevertheless, this migration has also given Cultural Studies – and by extension, critical
theory, philosophy, literature and the theoretical humanities more generally – pause
for *renewed* reflection upon the reduction of (qualitative) thought to (quantitative)
product, (critical) education to (utilitarian) skill-set, and ultimately upon the
im/possibility of its own institutional embeddedness.

Of course, these reflections are only novel in part. Whilst we must pay heed to – and
indeed intervene in – the singularities of these processes (the modes of 'coercive
accountability' now dominant but veiled in silence) we cannot lose sight of the fact
that 'critical' thought (in its Kantian, Marxist or extended modes) has always dwelled

parallax
ISSN 1353-4645 print/ISSN 1460-700X online © 2004 Taylor & Francis Ltd
http://www.tandf.co.uk/journals
DOI: 10.1080/1353464042000208477

within/without an academic/conceptual/economic structure it calls into question, throwing open the 'originary' contradictions, difficulties and challenges that inhere in such a dwelling. In part at least, this issue of **parallax** is an attempt to accede to these difficulties and challenges, without smoothing over the contradictions, and to negotiate between the singular and the general, without forging a too easy rapprochement.

The *call* for papers for this issue invited contributors to address how those working within (and without?) the academy are to provide and maintain 'spaces' for (critical) thought – (fully) funded (institutional) structures etc. – within (and without?) an academy increasingly saturated by an ethos of measurement, calculation, commodification and control of teaching, research and thought. What might it mean to think (critically) both within/without and *about* the academy in the face of such contemporary developments, and how might we articulate them with(in) the broader debates surrounding instrumental rationality, bureaucratic control, governmentality and the archive?

With these broad goals in mind, the texts assembled here spill out beyond the institutional state of Cultural Studies and critical theory in Britain to engage with other disciplines (anthropology, philosophy, literature, politics, etc.); other theoretical discourses (deconstruction, critical pedagogy and/in the university); other – regrettably limited – geographies/places/spaces (Canada, America, Austria, Australia, etc.[5]); other histories (of [the ideas of] the university, pedagogy, technology, curriculum, performance, management, citizenship, nationalism, democracy, Statehood, and so forth, more generally, combined with the singular histories carried under these rubrics), and finally – always, of course, a strategic finality – other expanded means of conceptualising an 'auditing of culture' (playing on both sides of the genitive): (a) culture that is both audit*ed* and audit*s*, (a) culture that risks taking '*responsibility* for the audibility of the numb'.[6]

For their help in producing this issue of **parallax** we would like to thank the production team at Taylor and Francis – for their guidance and efforts – our arts and reviews editors, Lynn Turner and Marcel Swiboda – for their expertise and time – Thorsten Schimmel – for his permission to reproduce one of the 'Silentium' series on our front cover – and, of course, all of the contributors, without whom etc. etc.

Peter Kilroy, Rowan Bailey and Nicholas Chare

Notes

[1] 'Research Assessment Exercise'.
[2] For the details of this closure, and its relationship to the mechanisms of the R.A.E., see Shore and Wright in this volume.
[3] To borrow Shore and Wright's phrase in this volume and elsewhere.

[4] See Timothy Clark and Nicholas Royle, 'Editorial Audit', *Oxford Literary Review*, 17:1–2 (1995), p.4.
[5] Not all locations exhibit an equally interventionist State, nor do their modes of accountability equally resemble one another or bear the same name.
[6] See Bauman, *Life in Fragments* (Oxford: Blackwell, 1995), pp.241–242.

parallax, 2004, vol. 10, no. 2, 3–18

Auditing Derrida

Simon Morgan Wortham

I. Balancing the books

Without the least knowledge of the other contributions to this issue of *parallax*, I am certain I will not be alone in drawing attention to the range of meanings, the polysemic gamut, of this word 'audit'. 'Audit', 'auditory', 'auditorium': in the first place, it puts us in the lexical and etymological vicinity of a *hearing*, and therefore an audience. To audit is to examine, to reckon (reckon up, reckon upon or reckon with), but also, inseparably, it is to *hear*. An audit can be defined, for example, as an examination of accounts (in the OED, a 'periodical settlement of accounts', a 'solemn rendering of accounts') *by reference to witnesses*. Thus, an audit unavoidably entails a space (or spaces), a procedure or protocol, a process or structure, that is inextricably linked to the auratic, to the juridical, and especially to a certain theatricality, each in turn being closely connected to the other. As a hearing, or in its irreducible relation to a hearing (this 'other' term hidden within itself), an audit ultimately cannot suppose or uphold its own self-contained space or logic of identity, and by extension it cannot without a certain irony assert a consistent principle or set of principles at work, a pure 'systematicity' being rigorously upheld, a formally reliable 'internal' mechanism or methodology being confidently put in place. Instead, it simply must call for, or address itself to, or take its cue from the *other*. Of course, the various derivations of this little word 'audit' frequently imply the attempt to restrict, determine, institutionalize – and thereby stabilize – the space of what is 'auditable'. Yet, notwithstanding this obvious fact, it is precisely in this very same context that a 'relation', a call, an address to the (ear of the) other becomes indispensable. The 'auditable' is thus framed by a space whose borders are marked by the trait of a certain deconstructibility, by a limit which is continually dislocated at the very moment the audit seeks to impose and define itself, to make itself at home in this or that particular place, to assert territorial rights. The situation of audit, including the irreducible supplement of a *hearing* (in the confines of an auditorium, perhaps), would therefore obey the law of the parergon, whereby the delineation of the aesthetic form of the work, and by extension the identity of the object of cognition, turns out to depend upon the contour, border or frame as its enabling condition. The constitutive function which the frame thereby acquires makes it an indispensable element in the composition of the object's 'form', so that it cannot in turn be located so decisively as just the limit of the object, merely the 'outer' edge of its formal properties. And, as Samuel Weber has told us, 'just this participation' of the *other* in the Same 'would require another frame',[1] not least if the 'auditable' is therefore to continue taking *place* at all. And then, as this frame once more partakes of

parallax
ISSN 1353-4645 print/ISSN 1460-700X online © 2004 Taylor & Francis Ltd
http://www.tandf.co.uk/journals
DOI: 10.1080/1353464042000208486

its constitutive function as an indispensable element in the composition of the 'thing' in question, *another*. And then *another*... Such a situation, for Weber, comes close to describing what he means by theatricality (without, of course, giving it a simple form). An ongoing goings-on, a ceaseless dislocation which puts place continually into play. And which, at every turn, not only profoundly disorients the distinction between the 'actors' and 'audience' (in and of an audit, for example), but which also fundamentally undermines the taking of a disinterested, extraterritorial position – a standpoint – from which one might attempt judgement itself.

From this point of view – one which links the audit to a certain (one might say, impossible) territorialization of space as place, or a theatrical goings-on – the figure of the Auditor might nevertheless recall Heidegger's technological man, who 'in the midst of beings [*physis*] to which he is exposed [*ausgesetzt*], seeks to gain a stand and to establish himself' by means of a 'process of mastering beings', a process which is 'supported and guided by a knowledge of beings. This *knowledge* is called *techne*'.[2] In the university, however, it is no easy matter to gain a stand, as Derrida, reading Kant, has shown us. (I'm going over old ground here. You may have heard this one before.) In 'Mochlos', Derrida suggests that, just as the founding of the law cannot simply be a juridical question or matter, one either of legality or of illegality, so the founding of the university cannot merely be treated as a 'university event', bearing instead a kind of structural relation to an alterity which in fact precedes the distinction between the 'inside' and the 'outside' of the university 'itself'. Since 'there can be no pure concept of the university [...] due very simply to the fact that the university is *founded*',[3] a legitimation crisis arises and imposes itself from the outset, one which also raises the question of orientation in and for the university. Through a close reading of Kant's *The Conflict of the Faculties*, Derrida suggests that Kant attempts to contain and control the violently disruptive and divisive energies of this intractable crisis by reducing it, localizing it, insisting on its nature as mere 'conflict' rather than out-and-out 'war'. Thus, as Derrida puts it, Kant 'propos[es] for it a solution that is properly "parliamentary"'[4]: the university is reconceived as a 'faculty parliament'. In this solution, the higher faculties (theology, law, medicine) occupy the right bench and defend the statutes of government, while the left bench is occupied by the philosophy faculty which offers 'rigorous examinations and objections' in the name and pursuit of truth. The opposition that results from this 'parliamentary solution' for Kant serves the higher purposes of a 'free system of government' and therefore resolves conflict into a more fundamental image of unity and accord. However, borrowing from Kant's own essay, 'What is Orientation in Thinking?', Derrida points out that right and left are not classified or recognized according to 'a conceptual or logical determination' but only from 'a sensory topology that has to be referred to the subjective position of the human body'.[5] This means that as 'directions' left and right cannot be fixed in universal terms according to incontrovertible logical determinants or objective principles, so that the 'parliamentary' opposition between left and right into which the university's conflicts are projected and attemptedly resolved by Kant offers a no more reliable source of orientation for the university. As Timothy Bahti has put it, 'when we use corporeal directions we mean, "Be like me"',[6] and therefore we address the other's right as if it were a left, the other's left as if it were a right. The resultant confusions between my left and another's right potentialized by this situation can be located not just in the subjective position of the human body, of course, but also in the sensory orientations collectively of parliamentary members within a body politic of modern, democratic, Western society developing after Kant. Thus, as Bahti points out with regard to certain modern institutions of government, 'in the parliamentary situation, the left – the "opposition" – is located from the perspective of the president or the speaker, but the speaker's left is obviously the left's right'.[7] Just at the point of seeking direction, then, the body (the 'parliamentary' body of the university, for example) is suddenly disoriented, unbalanced, off-balance. Where exactly *are* we? In the university, technological man – Audit Man – indeed struggles to find his place or gain a stand. And so the idea of a 'balance-sheet' so closely connected to the dictionary definition of our little word 'audit' occasions a small burst of laughter.

II. The ear of the other

But perhaps (for a laugh?) we should try to *audit* deconstruction or Derrida. First of all, this means we should try to *hear* him. But how would one go about auditing or hearing Derrida?

At the beginning of 'Otobiographies', itself a text originally presented as a lecture at the University of Montreal in 1979 and followed by roundtable discussions (an audit?) in which a select assembly of distinguished colleagues participated, Derrida has this to say:

> I would like to spare you the tedium, the waste of time, and the subservience that always accompany the classic pedagogical procedures of forging links, referring back to prior premises or arguments, justifying one's own trajectory, method, system, and more or less skillful transitions, reestablishing continuity, and so on. These are but some of the imperatives of classical pedagogy with which, to be sure, one can never break once and for all. Yet, if you were to submit to them rigorously, they would very soon reduce you to silence, tautology, and tiresome repetition.[8]

For Derrida, it is neither that the academic conventions of a more or less orthodox pedagogy can simply be ignored, surpassed or abandoned, nor that they permit themselves to be unquestioningly defended and thereby unproblematically reproduced. In other words, they can't just be adopted or assumed as a shared set of conventions permitting reliable auditability, but nor can they be rejected, critiqued, comprehended or otherwise *calculated* from an extraterritorial vantage point. Rather, any teaching necessarily partaking of pedagogical tradition that tries none the less to remain wholeheartedly devoted to an unsupplemented reinscription or conservation of the method or the system that allows and enables it to set out will inevitably dwindle into circularly self-justifying practices that actually inhibit and eventually preclude everything to do with the *event* of (a) teaching: of teaching as a singularly performative activity and a finally incalculable form of address to – but, perhaps more so, *from* – the other, an other that ultimately exceeds or outstrips the dialogical engagement it invites. One can therefore neither simply take nor leave 'classic pedagogical procedures', and in fact one must to some extent both take (partake of) and leave them at one and the same time in order for teaching to take place at all: parergonal double-bind again. (On closer inspection, then, Derrida's remarks – flippant or jokey though they might sound on first hearing – would in fact seem to raise important questions concerning the (im)possibility of a responsible standpoint on quite difficult and complex issues having to do with teaching and accountability or auditability.) In the face of this complication of otherwise easily polarizable positions on the issue of pedagogical tradition, Derrida therefore proposes a 'compromise' to his audience. This has to do with a deconstructive procedure that presents its practitioner as engaged in some sort of settling of accounts on a number of problems (however ironic or impossible this may seem, it is of course also unavoidable), rather than aspiring to the teaching of 'truth' as such. Derrida anticipates that, for some, such an approach will seem too 'aphoristic or inadmissible', while others will accept it as 'law', and yet others will 'judge [it] to be not quite aphoristic enough'.[9] While it would be easy enough to translate such categorizations into very familiar groupings, perspectives or positions according to which deconstruction is routinely 'audited', what is perhaps more interesting here is that, on the basis of just this 'compromise', whereby deconstruction presents itself as neither just entirely inside nor outside 'classical pedagogy', Derrida begins to question or, one might even say, *recalculate* 'otherwise' the possibilities of academic freedom in the very process of what would seem to be an appeal to it.

Derrida insists that, since he does not wish to 'transform myself into a diaphanous mouthpiece of eternal pedagogy',[10] a fountain of self-proclaimed truth, untrammelled authority and self-sustaining mastery (Derrida himself already having indicated the inevitable atrophying of any such teaching, although also its unavoidable persistence to some extent), his 'compromise' or procedure is therefore one that would seem to somewhat liberate his audience or the 'students' of his teaching, so that 'whoever no longer wishes to follow may do so'.[11] 'As everyone knows, by the terms of *academic freedom* – I repeat: a-ca-dem-ic free-dom – you can take it or leave it', he says.[12] Here, Derrida not only alerts our attention to the somewhat contradictory elements inscribed within our usual evocations of pedagogical tradition, which stress both teacherly authority and freedom of inquiry. More than this, a certain ironic tone becomes evident, underlying what seems to be a quite deliberately repeated and emphasized insistence on academic freedom itself. For Derrida has already shown that any worthwhile teaching (such as deconstruction, for instance), positioned in an ambivalent or equivocal relation to 'classical pedagogy', neither simply frees nor binds the event or activity of (a) teaching in relation to (a) tradition. Derrida's (teaching of) deconstruction in regard to the teaching of Nietzsche obviously cannot offer a straightforward choice to the audience or student of Derrida, between unencumbered intellectual freedom, on the one hand, or absolute bondage to pedagogical mastery, on the other. Just as Derrida, by his own admission, can neither simply take nor leave 'classical pedagogy', and (for that matter) since any teaching worth the name must both take and leave it simultaneously, so those that hear Derrida speak at Montreal in 1979 would, similarly, finally be bereft of any such choice forming the basis of a conventional appeal to academic freedom. To agree with everything Derrida would have to say, to 'take' deconstruction in undiluted form, would be to absolutely submit to, to repeat in the most conventional way, and thereby necessarily to obliterate its teaching: that is, ultimately, *to take leave of it*. On the other hand, to absolutely reject or wholly take issue with, to entirely take leave of Derrida's discussion or approach from the outset would necessitate, quite impossibly, either a complete departure from the conventions of academic exposition which Derrida insists constitute the minimal level of intelligibility of his (or indeed any other) learned address, or otherwise would manifest an absolute defence of 'classical pedagogy' – in which case any dispute with Derrida, any supposed 'taking leave' of him, could never take the form of an absolutely diametrical opposition, for reasons he himself already presupposes and makes clear. One can therefore never simply 'take it or leave it' in regard to Derrida's lecture, or for that matter in regard to the teaching of deconstruction, perhaps even teaching itself, in general. (Problem yet again of the parergon, of theatricality, of judgement, of audit.) Thus, it is not just that 'classical pedagogy' and 'academic freedom' as clearly identifiable categories or forms constitute contradictory or somewhat opposed elements that vie with one another, bringing an awkward tension to bear on accepted notions and norms concerning scholarly tradition and convention. Rather, it is that *both* 'academic freedom' and 'classical pedagogy' are themselves traversed or cross-cut by differential traits that actually, paradoxically bind them together according to the logic of the supplement, of the remainder, or of the double bind. An incalculable series. Just as Derrida takes the stand, then, it's difficult to reckon with or count upon the event which takes place here, or to audit what one hears… and this demands from us a different kind of response and responsibility. Being able neither to simply take it or leave it leaves us in the impossible yet necessary space we might associate with the kind of dissensual academic community advocated recently by critics like Bill Readings and J. Hillis Miller. This would be a (so-called) community not simply bounded by a horizon of consensus and sustained by the sort of communicative rationality advocated by the German Idealists or, more recently, Habermasian thought; nor would it be a community underpinned by freedom of dissent as a notion indissociable from traditional claims to academic freedom – a notion which in fact presupposes at the more fundamental level an entirely common and shared understanding of academic protocols and conventions. Dissensus of the kind that leaves all those engaged in the scene of teaching unable to either take it or leave it obviously implies a complicated network of relations and obligations which nevertheless *leaves open* the question of responsibility or of the 'ethical' (even as an impossible one), precisely because, in the very event of teaching, such a question remains irreducible to the rationality and rational ground of autonomous subjects, or of *the* (taken-for-granted) autonomous subject. This opens an impossible yet necessary (theatrical or parergonal) space, therefore, in which responsibility, obligation, indebtedness, accountability or auditability all need to be calculated 'otherwise', heard (audited) with the ear of the other.

III. 'Where there is evidence, there is not testimony'

The idea of the audit as a *hearing* suggests two concepts, themes or motifs which appear to be closely related but, as Derrida points out, may in fact be incommensurable with one another: evidence and testimony. Of course, evidence – an 'evidence-based approach' – is one of the mainstays of the current Quality agenda, which itself serves to refine and further operationalize the ethos of Excellence. And, of course, evidence and testimony when taken together form a crucial part of a juridical technique or technics which includes the theatrical and the auditory. Taking the stand, as much as taking a stand!

Testimony and evidence, then, seem to go hand in hand. But let's hear Derrida once more, during an interview with Bernard Steigler conducted in 1993:

> A testimony has never been or should never be mistaken for evidence. Testimony, in the strict sense of the term, is advanced in the first person by someone who says, 'I swear,' who pledges to tell the truth, gives his word, and asks to be taken at his word in a situation where nothing has been proven – where nothing will ever be proven, for structural reasons, for reasons that are essential and not contingent. It is possible for testimony to be corroborated by evidence, but the process of evidence is absolutely heterogeneous to that of testimony, which implies faith, belief, sworn faith, the pledge to tell the truth, the 'I swear to tell the truth, the whole truth and nothing but the truth.' Consequently, where there is evidence, there is not testimony. The technical archive, in principle, should never replace testimony. It may furnish exhibits or evidence, within the theoretical order that is the order of evidence, and must be foreign to the element of credit, faith, or belief implied by the testimonial pledge.[13]

The example Derrida uses to illustrate this idea of the heterogeneity and structural incompatibility of evidence and testimony is the Rodney King verdict, after the 1991 trial in Los Angeles which concerned police brutality and racism. The videotape of King's beating may well have served 'as an exhibit, perhaps as evidence, but it did not replace testimony'[14] – and in fact it was inadmissible as testimony, so that the young man who held the video camera was himself required to attend the trial, take the stand, and swear before the jury and the court 'that it was really he who held the camera, that he was present at the scene, that he saw what he shot'.[15] The technical recording could not count as testimony in its own right: the hearing needed to *hear* the testimony of an 'I swear to tell the truth, the whole truth and nothing but the truth'. 'Technics will never produce a testimony',[16] Derrida therefore concludes (illustrated here by the technology of the video recorder). On the other hand, however, testimony:

> as witness *borne*, as attestation, always consists in discourse. To be a witness consists in seeing, in hearing, etc., but to bear witness is always to speak, to engage in and uphold, to sign a discourse. It is not possible to bear witness without a discourse. Well, this discourse itself already harbors technics, even if only in the form of this iterability implied by the oath, to say nothing of this technics already constituted by the minimal grammaticality or rhetoricality which an attestation requires. Hence the apparent contradiction: technics will never make a testimony, testimony is pure of any technics, and yet it is impure, and yet it already implies the appeal to technics.[17]

Now, it strikes me that the 'audit culture' affecting higher education today, along with other public (and indeed private) institutions and organizations, reconfigures the relations between evidence and testimony in very specific ways. In the first place, although we began by insisting that an audit, right down to its etymological and lexical roots, irreducibly implies a *hearing*, nevertheless it seems impossible to deny that today's 'audit culture' tries its best to minimize testimony at the expense of evidence. In a sense, this suggests an effort to somehow dilute the juridical effect or quality of its proceedings, to detheatricalize and deauralize the audit. Many of the bodies and agencies involved in today's audit culture have a vested interest in presenting themselves as engaged in something other than a *hearing*, and there are many people today who recognize that the supposedly benign and progressive attitudes underlying this kind of discourse only thinly conceal other motives which are all the more brutal for being surreptitious. In higher education institutions in Britain, therefore, the changing balance between testimony and evidence is illustrated by the fact that teaching is rarely if ever inspected these days. Instead, documentary evidence is techno-bureaucratically produced and assessed, both internally and externally. It is approved, archived, cross-referenced, checked for consistency and appropriacy, verified, disseminated, and thereby and thereafter tested as evidence alongside and against *itself* in such a way that the testamentary support offered in the past by the classroom, for example, is dispensed with as far as possible. Testimony, we might say, is no substitute for evidence these days. Testimony, hearing, the auratic, the juridical and the theatrical connotations and conditions of an audit – all of these must be diluted, minimized, excluded as far as possible, if the incalculable, aleatory and ambivalent effects so inimicable to the audit culture of today (those we've discussed already) are to be avoided.

However, this set of circumstances we're calling 'audit culture' represents less of a simple reversal of that which Derrida finds in the Rodney King trial (where evidence was no substitute for testimony) than a shift in the balance of forces between testimony and evidence taking place in a significantly different institutional and political setting, which similarly demonstrates a certain heterogeneity or incompatibility, a persistent tension or ongoing struggle between the two. For Derrida goes on to show that, while testimony and evidence simply cannot be harmoniously integrated or synthesized, they necessarily continue to function (non-symbiotically) as the irreducible supplement of one another. While there are those – on both sides of the debate – who would happily concur with the idea that the testamentary support of the teaching inspection is wholly alien to the technics of an 'evidence-based approach' to Quality and Excellence, nevertheless we should be reminded, on reading or hearing Derrida in this (video recorded) interview from 1993, that just as testimony functions *as* testimony only by recourse to the evidentiary structures of writing, recording and therefore technics, so 'evidence' can never be pure of, can never simply take leave of, testimony. Try as it might to avoid everything associated with the structure and effects of the testamentary, right down to and including the signature (which of these so-called 'Quality' documents are ever signed by anyone? – their mode of verification, validation or authentification is instead by reference to other documents, which are in turn verified and authenticated by reference to others still), testimony is *part* of evidence to the extent that, as Derrida tells us, the testament is bound to drift into the technical domain characterized by the evidentiary. Testimony is destined to contaminate evidence, since it cannot ever avoid being contaminated *by* or becoming evidence in all its technical manifestations (one thinks of outlines of seminar sessions in course handbooks, records of staff-student committee meetings, staff appraisals and other minutes, all of which in different ways carry testimony into the evidentiary). Hence, on closer inspection (ha ha) it is not just the case that 'where there is evidence, there is not testimony'. The radical heterogeneity or incompatibility of the two far from preclude testimony becoming evidence or, for that matter, evidence ('the technical archive') being drawn into a tension or struggle with the testimony that ceaselessly drifts its way. And what Derrida has to say about evidence and testimony suggests that this tension could never simply be pacified by diplomatic negotiation or accommodation, nor even dispelled by legal repatriation. So that, if testimony is bound to bother 'evidence', despite all its best efforts to the contrary, then, by extension, the 'evidence-based approach' of Quality and Excellence can never hope to avoid parergonal effects of the auratic, the theatrical, the juridical. The audit can never so decisively distinguish itself from a *hearing* after all. It may well try to obliterate its own signature, but in the end it cannot wholly avoid *witness* or *witnesses*. A hearing after all, then: and who will be the judge of that? (Always an *other*?)

IV. Archive fever

Audit culture seems to imply archive fever. Since, as we've just seen, every discourse, including that of testimony, is prone to a technics of inscription and archivization, it comes as no surprise that in *Archive Fever* Derrida shows how the history of psychoanalysis is not only the history contained in its archival records, but that psychoanalysis is more fundamentally the history *of* its very archivization. For psychoanalysis – as a machine for the analysis of testimony – is also nothing less than archival thinking itself, archivo-analysis, archive fever. Achivization doesn't just come afterwards, even as an unavoidable contingency, but instead constitutes the very hallmark of the psychoanalytic. This archivization of psychoanalysis, then, is in turn 'determined by a state of the technology of communication'[18] which does not merely lie on the *outside* of psychoanalysis. On the other hand, however, neither is this 'state' just on the 'inside' of psychoanalysis as its internal, formal, essential characteristic or property. Instead, the very formation and character of psychoanalysis as archivo-analysis is irreducibly linked, Derrida tells us, to the technical and technological conditions surrounding archivization in Freud's time:

> One can dream or speculate about the geo-techno-logical shocks which would have made the landscape of the psychoanalytic archive unrecognizable for the past century if, to limit myself to these indications, Freud, his contemporaries, collaborators and immediate disciples, instead of writing thousands of letters by hand, had had access to MCI or AT&T telephonic credit cards, portable tape recorders, computers, printers, faxes, televisions, teleconferences, and above all E-mail [...] I will limit myself to a mechanical remark: this archival earthquake would not have limited its effects to the *secondary recording*, to the printing and conservation of the history of psychoanalysis. It would have transformed this history from top to bottom and in the most initial inside of its production, in its very *events* [...] The archivization produces as much as it records the event.[19]

We might wonder about the implications of this historical shift for audit culture today, particularly in the sense that such a shift threatens to render 'unrecognizable' the technical substrate of the evidentiary upon which it relies (what happens when serial versions of Quality documents circulate and proliferate by e-mail correspondence and e-mail attachment within the institution, for instance?). Be that as it may, one writing machine that psychoanalysis is able to consider in its own day is the *Mystic Pad* (*der Wunderblock*). We might consider this, Derrida tells us, 'a technical model of a machine tool, intended, in Freud's eyes, to *represent on the outside* memory as *internal archivization*'.[20] However, referring to his earlier text, 'Freud and the Scene of Writing', Derrida reminds us that:

> Freud does not explicitly examine the status of the 'materialized' supplement which is necessary to the alleged spontaneity of memory, even if that spontaneity were differentiated in itself, thwarted by a censorship or repression which, moreover, could not act on a perfectly spontaneous memory. Far from the machine being a pure absence of spontaneity, its *resemblance* to the psychical apparatus, its existence and its necessity bear witness to the finitude of the mnemic spontaneity which is thus supplemented. The machine – and, consequently, representation – is death and finitude within the psyche.[21]

For Derrida, then, the machine is death and finitude within the psyche and therefore the death drive is at the origin of the Freudian archive, it is the 'original proposition', the latest news, which stops psychoanalysis becoming 'a lot of ink and paper for nothing', a secondary body of evidence, an unoriginal technology, an empty-handed writing which ultimately says nothing, or nothing new.[22] Yet the death drive is simultaneously that which 'not only incites forgetfulness, amnesia, the annihilation of memory, as *mneme* or to *anamnesis*, but also commands the radical effacement, in truth the eradication, of that which can never be reduced to *mneme* or *anamnesis*, that is the archive, consignation, the documentary or monumental apparatus as *hypomnema*, mnemotechnical supplement or representative, auxiliary or memorandum'.[23] The otherwise 'apparently useless expenditure of paper, ink, and typographic printing' accompanying the production of the psychoanalytic archive is only justified, insofar as Freud is concerned, by 'putting forward the novelty of his discovery', that of the death drive, the 'silent vocation' of which is to 'burn the archive', 'incite amnesia', and thereby refute 'the economic principle' of the archive as 'accumulation and capitalization of memory on some substrate and in an exterior place'.[24] In this sense, the *Mystic Pad* is itself the originary supplement or prosthetic of the Freudian archive, or of psycho-archivo-analysis, or of psycho-archivo-fever. It is not just part of a 'secondary' technical machinery that comes afterwards. Moreover, this also implies once more that the fever which causes the psychoanalytic archive to *burn* doesn't just belong to psychoanalysis as its 'internal' property or as an essential (psychic/non-technical) character trait. For this archive fever yet again burns the very distinction between the 'inside' and 'outside' of psychoanalysis. Thus, if the death drive leaves psychoanalysis empty-handed, burnt up with a fever, causing the archive to always work '*a priori*, against itself',[25] then the death-driven archivization which causes the archive to burn so feverishly cannot simply be limited to psychoanalysis 'itself'. And if Derrida's *Archive Fever* is the paper or taper which sets the archive ablaze beyond psychoanalysis 'itself', today's audit culture lies no more on the outside of the double-bind which this book details, than testimony lies purely on the outside of an uncontaminated body of evidence. Archive fever is death-driven, all the time destroying what it produces, with a feverishness that is more akin – or more conducive – to laughter than to a 'solemn rendering of accounts'.

V. The age of audit

In *The University in Ruins*, Bill Readings suggests the decline, at the end of the twentieth century, of long-standing expressivist or synecdochic relations between individual and community, discipline and university and, crucially, university and nation-state. These kind of relations underpin the thinking of, for example, the 'human', the 'social' and the determination of 'rights' as an expression of modernity after Enlightenment. It is such a decline which therefore brings about the erosion of a notion of communicative community in the university as advocated by the German Idealists, one that founds a tradition of the very Idea of the university which runs all the way through to the likes of Habermas. Amid the ruins of communicative community, then, Readings envisages the possibilities of this 'community of dissensus', as he terms it. This – perhaps impossibly fluid – grouping would found itself on a rather groundless commitment to 'thinking without identity'.[26] The midwife, or parent even, of such a dissensual community would be none other than the 'dereferentialised' University of Excellence itself, now utterly Idea-less, a machine geared entirely to its own optimal performance, without any concern for the grounding and coherence of its contents. Yet such a community of dissensus, insofar as it would be characterized by the activity of 'thinking without identity', could only produce research findings and 'objects' for study that were 'systematically incapable of closure'.[27] Thus it would necessarily be incompatible with the strictly calibrated measure of Excellence. Yet the dissensual community would, again, therefore not simply be a dissenting one, engaged in full-frontal opposition with regard to today's academic institutions. As a product or offspring of the ruined university of Excellence, it would mark and re-mark the disoriented non-self-identicality of the contemporary institution, its incommensurability with itself. This would not only mean that the evaluative thinking of dissensual communities would transvalue the evaluations of Excellence. It would demonstrate the 'out-of-joint-ness' of Excellence with itself.

In other words, the University of Excellence seems to have two left feet. Excellence/ dissensus constitutes a non-self-identical double: this 'pair', if it is one, suggests the two left (or two right) footedness of the university today. The university takes its stand only to 'walk on two feet', undecidably two left or two right feet: just the motif Derrida has used, in 'Mochlos', to describe the (disoriented) founding and footing of the Enlightenment university as a 'parliamentary faculty' envisaged by Kant in *The Conflict of the Faculties*. In this sense, the University of Excellence was always going to deliver old news. News which is already as old, then, as Kant. Or, to risk alluding to a too familiar pairing, which is older than Hegel. But, then again, what is the age of Hegel?:

> '[...] and if I may be permitted to evoke my own experience [...] I remember having learned, in my twelfth year – destined as I was to enter the theological seminary of my country – Wolf's definitions of the so-called idea clara and that, in my fourteenth year, I had assimilated all the figures and rules of syllogism. And I still know them'.

And he still knows them.

Hegel in his twelfth year. You can see the scene from here.[28]

This is Derrida, in 1986, on the first page of his essay 'The Age of Hegel', quoting Hegel's letter of April 16, 1822, 'To the Royal Ministry of Spiritual, Academic, and Medical Affairs'. While writing, Hegel remembers an age or a time between his twelfth year, when he's eleven, and his fourteenth year, when he's thirteen: a time when he's twelve! A lot of dates and numbers to reckon with, but can we reliably count (on) them? (Hegel's also fifty-two here; that is, when he writes the letter. Exactly from *where*, then, do we 'see the scene', this little piece of theatre contrived by philosophers or philosophy?). One minute we're adding, the next subtracting, to count precisely upon the coincidence of the number with the age. Yet Excellence counts on just this coincidence of the age – its own age – with the number, the points score, the teaching or research rating of an institution. The R.A.E., for example, is an adding machine in and of the age of Excellence.

Going back to Hegel, all these complex calculations are going on in a letter to the Ministry of Spiritual, Academic and Medical Affairs. The letter is part of a special report commissioned by the Ministry, 'by a State bureaucracy in the process of organizing the nationalization of the structures of philosophical education by extracting it, based on a historical compromise, from clerical jurisdiction', as Derrida reminds us.[29] Not just a 'minor' text, then, but a significant landmark in a statist problematics of education, or of modernity's institution of reason. While Hegel may well have thought that the rationality of philosophical instruction might 'culminate most universally and most powerfully in the concept of the State',[30] his recollection of (the age of) childhood, and of the 'already-not-yet' of philosophy – at once a matter of private confidence, philosophical demonstration and public address (Hegel is at once already a philosopher, engaged in philosophy, and not yet a true philosopher, learning mechanically by rote, at twelve) – this recollection finds Hegel foundering, in the manner of an 'already-not yet': 'advancing or foundering, with more or less confidence, in the techno-bureaucratic space of a highly determined State', says Derrida. A State to come, for philosophy or by way of philosophy, which, for philosophy, nevertheless already *is*, as the letter itself presupposes. In such a state, in relation to such a State (which, according to a somewhat maddening temporality, 'already-is-to-come'), it is no wonder that Hegel advances and founders at once, to's and fro's, 'with more or less confidence' (with two left feet?). Again, we might remark the simultaneity of this 'more' and 'less', the simultaneity of addition and deduction as the characteristic feature of an apparently (although only apparently) self-same state, the state (State) of Hegel, which has everything to do with his age. In letters to the Minister written during the same period, Hegel frets over the State's provision for him in his old age, and for the family after his death. Hegel is in a state, when he thinks of his age (now adding years on instead of taking them away, although still during the same period of 1822, of course), and he wants – however impossibly – to be definite about numbers, specifically about sums (fittingly, though, these are described by Hegel as 'supplementary revenues'). He wants to be sure about – to audit – his currency (in both a broad and narrow sense) with the State.

Narrowly, he wants assurances of money for the future (i.e. insurance), in the interests, supposedly, of future philosophical research. 'I dare anticipate the realization of these benevolent promises only in connection with Your Excellency's noble plans for the development of knowledge and the education of the young, and I regard the improvement of my own economic situation only as a subordinate element in this totality', writes Hegel.[31] (Sounds like an application for external funding today!). But how can one be sure that the age of Hegel, or indeed of philosophy, is indeed *current* with the State (or, indeed, the state) Hegel finds himself in, 'advancing' and 'foundering', more or less? A State or state that 'already-is-to-come'? And, of course, this moment of a State-sponsored, techno-bureaucratic institutional reformation of philosophical education doesn't just belong to the age of Hegel. It also relates to the age of Derrida, and to his involvement with the GREPH during the 1980s, going towards a report to the French government on the reformation of philosophy's pedagogy and institution; the latter involving the question of the 'proper' age of a philosophical education, in at least its double sense – forming more or less the brunt of 'The Age of Hegel'.[32] Furthermore it's not just the age of Derrida that's involved here. Rather, where the techno-bureaucratic institutional reform of education, including philosophy, is concerned, all this relates to our age, too, the age of Excellence, Quality, audit culture, and the R.A.E., all of which I would call – appropriately enough, by missorting the letters – 'Raelity'. And no doubt, it relates also to the future, the future R.A.E., and beyond. 'Already-not-yet': is this temporality, already, or yet (not yet), Hegelian?

'There is a Hegelian hierarchization, but it is circular, and the minor is always carried, sublated [...] beyond the opposition, beyond the limit of inside and outside in(to) the major. And inversely. The potency of this age without age derives from this great empirico-philosophical cycle'.[33] And yet, according to the temporality at work in the vicinity of Derrida's reflections on 'The Age of Hegel', we do not seem to be able to count on things ever coming full-circle within a self-realizing totality. (As I'll suggest in a moment, R is never quite R.) Nevertheless, the doubling which occurs in the formulation 'age without age' is itself telling, as it posits a repetition with a difference, indicated of course by the preposition 'without'. Far from underlining an atemporal structure or cycle of recurrence, 'age without age' in fact suggests here the non-self-identicality or non-coincidence of the 'age' of Hegel with itself, a sharply disjointed temporality, along the lines perhaps of the missorted letters and the miscalculated sequence or sequentiality of Raelity.

But let's go back to R. 'On, then, on to R': remember Ramsay in Woolf's *To the Lighthouse*? Eighteenth letter of the alphabet. A number, therefore, by which we calculate another coming of age. Manhood perhaps (Law of the Father). First letter of (the age of) Raelity, when (albeit by dint of a missort) we all grow up and face today's realities, the realities of audit. On, then, on, from the philosophical mind and memory of H. to the 'splendid mind' of R.:

> For if thought is like the keyboard of a piano, divided into so many notes, or like the alphabet is ranged in twenty-six letters all in order, then his splendid mind had no sort of difficulty in running over those letters one by one, firmly and accurately, until it had reached, say, the

letter Q. He reached Q. Very few people in the whole of England ever reach Q [...] But after Q? What comes next? After Q there are a number of letters the last of which is scarcely visible to mortal eyes, but glimmers red in the distance. Z is only reached once by one man in a generation. Still, if he could reach R it would be something. Here at least was Q. He dug his heels in at Q. Q he was sure of. Q he could demonstrate. If Q then is Q - R - Here he knocked his pipe out, with two or three resonant taps on the ram's horn which made the handle of the urn, and proceeded. 'Then R [...]' He braced himself. He clenched himself [...] A shutter, like the leathern eyelid of a lizard, flickered over the intensity of his gaze and obscured the letter R. In that flash of darkness he heard people saying – he was a failure – that R was beyond him. He would never reach R. On to R, once more. R - .[34]

Perhaps like an R.A.E. panellist engaged in the activity of auditing academic output, Mr Ramsay hopes to have 'no sort of difficulty', no difficulty of any sort, in sorting letters, not just letters of the kind sent by Hegel, but papers, made up of letters and sent as if they were letters, together with covering letters, to the panels of the R.A.E. For Ramsay, the number of letters are ranged 'all in order', from A to Z. Although, of course, 'on, then, on to R' always seems to entail a counter-movement, a counter-trajectory and temporality: 'back to Q'. A rather tiresome repetition, always going back, time and again, to Q. Progress stymied by a compulsion to repeat. To and fro between Q and R, on or back to R, which in the quoted passage doesn't always come after Q. Judgement of R is never simply judgement of R, then, but depends on the prior evaluation of Q. An evaluation (of Q) which in some sense is yet to come, or which in a certain way arrives after itself, only in the experience or moment of the judgement of R (which, of course, is not then the same as itself). R (i.e. Ramsay) is only 'sure' of Q at the moment he's 'on to R' (where certainty itself ends or is suspended). Time 'out of joint'. The number of letters, all ranged in order, with no difficulty of any sort, suddenly subjected to a missort. Not unlike Raelity itself.

Judgement of R (Ramsay) is never, then, simply judgement of R (the letter R). The letter collides yet never quite coincides with its recipient, never quite arrives in the capital (i.e. the initial of the proper name). Judgement of R is never simply judgement of R precisely because of this non-coincidence that characterizes their coincidence. Instead of a reassuring look in the mirror (R is R, therefore the sure identity of knowledge and the subject remains visibly intact), we have a disconcerting blink, right where it ought not to be, just where it was hoped to find the transparent, self-evident, self-identical grounds of knowledge ('If Q then is Q - R - '). 'A shutter, like the leathern eyelid of a lizard, flickered over the intensity of his gaze and obscured the letter R. In that flash of darkness he heard people saying – he was a failure – that R was beyond him. He would never reach R. On to R, once more. R - '.

Here is Derrida again, on or in the blink of an eye. Here he is, writing on the institution, on memory and sight, and on the question of the vision of the university, what is envisaged by the university, and so forth:

> Opening the eyes to know, closing them – or at least listening – in order to know how to learn and learn how to know: here we have a first sketch

of the rational animal. If the University is an institution for science and teaching, does it not have to go beyond memory and sight? In what rhythm? To hear and learn better, must it close its eyes or narrow its outlook? In cadence? What cadence? Shutting off sight in order to learn is of course only a figurative manner of speaking. No one will take it literally, and I am not proposing to cultivate an art of blinking. And I am resolutely in favour of a new University Enlightenment (*Aufklarung*). Still, I shall run the risk of extending my figuration a little farther, in Aristotle's company. In his *De anima* (421b) he distinguishes between man and those animals that have hard, dry eyes [*ton sklerophtalmon*], the animals lacking eyelids, the sort of sheath or tegumental membrane [*phragma*] which serves to protect the eye and permits it, at regular intervals, to close itself off in the darkness of inward thought or sleep. What is terrifying about an animal with hard eyes and a dry glance is that it always sees. Man can lower his sheath, adjust the diaphragm, narrow his sight, the better to listen, remember and learn. What might the University's diaphragm be?[35]

Here, Derrida implies that thought, learning, knowledge of any kind itself requires 'regular intervals' at which to pause, rest, evaluate. And the R.A.E., it goes without saying, comes at regular intervals, in order to undertake evaluation exercises. At night, in the dark, their relationship is an uncanny one, however. The 'intervals' which Derrida describes as vital to knowledge, learning and thought are precisely not characterized or presided over by the intensely unremitting stare of Ramsayesque 'hard, dry eyes' dedicated to the spectacle of transparent, self-evident self-identicality (Q is Q, R is R). While such a piercing gaze might suggest the punctual, punctuating, puncturing advent of the R.A.E., Derrida (long before time) reminds us that the 'interval' which actually facilitates thought, prompting us to evaluate knowledge, and to remember learning, is characterized by the blink of an eye, the passage of darkness. In this sense, Ramsay's failure, in a 'flash of darkness', would possibly (spectacularly) redeem itself. No need, then, to simply bemoan and wholly repudiate the intervention or insertion of the interval. But the interval will not just aid illumination or transparency, since it must also entail a suspension, a forgetting, a darkness, played out (against and within the light) according to the rhythms of a blink. The institution built on the principle of reason is also, if we follow Heidegger, built 'on what remains hidden in that principle', Derrida tells us, so that the 'principle of reason installs its empire only to the extent that the abyssal question of being that is hiding within it remains hidden, and with it the question of the grounding of the ground itself'.[36] Just as, in Derrida's 'Mochlos', the footing of the institution is found on uncertain foundations, so the vision of the university proceeds from what remains concealed. However, this raises the question of responsibility in that critics, professors, academics working at 'multiple sites [on] a stratified terrain' with 'postulations that are undergoing continual displacement' need to observe 'a sort of strategic rhythm' playing itself out between the 'barrier' and the 'abyss', between the protected horizon, the secured partition, of the university space and the invisible and unthought bottomless chasm on which this is founded. Yet this 'strategic rhythm' is, necessarily, ultimately incalculable, unforeseeable, and as such cannot ever merely be 'observed'. Indeed, it is the unprogrammability of this 'rhythm' which raises the very issue of a non-mechanical responsibility. As it pulsates unprogrammatically between the barrier (horizon of vision) and the abyss (hidden and unseen), this 'strategic rhythm' is therefore one that Derrida associates with 'the blinking of an eye'.[37]

Auditing Derrida, then, our hearing is always in a certain sense that of the *other*, our balance is 'off', we are in the midst of an impure yet undismissable testimony, the very age or time is more or less incalculable, the sequence is out, archive fever causes the 'economic principle' to burn. And in the vicinity of this quasi-comic juridico-theatrical space, we experience disorientation, we blink. But, after all, who would take this seriously? Whoever would propose to cultivate an art of blinking? Don't count on it!

Notes

[1] Samuel Weber, 'The Unraveling of Form', in A. Cholodenko [ed], *Mass Mediauras: Form, Technics, Media* (Stanford, CA: Stanford University Press, 1996), p.23.

[2] The translation here is found in Samuel Weber's essay, 'Upsetting the Setup: Remarks on Heidegger's "Questing After Technics"', in A. Cholodenko [ed], *Mass Mediauras: Form, Technics, Media* (Stanford, CA: Stanford University Press, 1996), pp.59–60. Weber translates from Martin Heidegger, *Nietzsche*, Bd. I (Pfullingun: Gunther Neske, 1961).

[3] Jacques Derrida, 'Mochlos', in Richard Rand [ed], *Logomachia: The Conflict of the Faculties* (Lincoln and London: University of Nebraska Press, 1992), p.29.

[4] Derrida, 'Mochlos', p.28.

[5] Derrida, 'Mochlos', p.31.

[6] Timothy Bahti, 'The Injured University', in Richard Rand [ed], *Logomachia: The Conflict of the Faculties* (Lincoln and London: University of Nebraska Press, 1992), p.62.

[7] Bahti, 'The Injured University', p.62

[8] Jacques Derrida, 'Otobiographies: The Teaching of Nietzsche and the Politics of the Proper Name', trans. Avital Ronell, in C. MacDonald [ed], *The Ear of the Other: Otobiography, Transference, Translation* (Lincoln and London: University of Nebraska Press, 1988), pp.3–4.

[9] Derrida, 'Otobiographies', p.4.

[10] Derrida, 'Otobiographies', p.4.

[11] Derrida, 'Otobiographies', p.4.

[12] Derrida, 'Otobiographies', p.4.

[13] Jacques Derrida and Bernard Stiegler, 'The Archive Market: Truth, Testimony, Evidence', in *Echographies of Television*, trans. Jennifer Bajorek (Cambridge: Polity Press, 2002), pp.93–4.

[14] Derrida and Stiegler, 'The Archive Market', p.94.

[15] Derrida and Stiegler, 'The Archive Market', p.94.

[16] Derrida and Stiegler, 'The Archive Market', p.94.

[17] Derrida and Stiegler, 'The Archive Market', pp.94–95.

[18] Jacques Derrida, *Archive Fever: A Freudian Impression*, trans. Eric Prenowitz (Chicago and London: University of Chicago Press, 1998), p.16.

[19] Derrida, *Archive Fever*, pp.16–17.

[20] Derrida, *Archive Fever*, p.13.

[21] Derrida's reference to 'Freud and the Scene of Writing' on p.14 of *Archive Fever* can be found in *Writing and Difference*, trans. Alan Bass (London: Routledge, 1978), pp.227–8.

[22] Derrida, *Archive Fever*, pp.8–9.

[23] Derrida, *Archive Fever*, p.11.

[24] Derrida, *Archive Fever*, p.12.

[25] Derrida, *Archive Fever*, p.12.

[26] Bill Readings, *The University in Ruins* (Cambridge, Mass. and London: Harvard University Press, 1996), p.127.

[27] Readings, *The University in Ruins*, p.128.

[28] Jacques Derrida, 'The Age of Hegel', in Samuel Weber [ed], *Demarcating the Disciplines: Philosophy, Literature, Art* (Minneapolis: University of Minnesota Press, 1986), p.1.

[29] Derrida, 'The Age of Hegel', p.4.

[30] Derrida, 'The Age of Hegel', p.5.

[31] Derrida, 'The Age of Hegel', p.13.

[32] The GREPH had been 'quick to criticize' the practice, inherited in a certain way from Hegel's imperatives, of 'beginning with teaching the content of knowledge, before even thinking it' – a teaching based on a mechanistic memorization as the prephilosophical pedagogic mode, which in turn assures 'a highly determined prephilosophical inculcation'. Derrida, 'The Age of Hegel', p.26. For Derrida, such pedagogy is deeply inscribed and engrained as part of the statist problematics of education within modernity, denying or postponing (in the Hegelian version, among others) 'access to thought – in its speculative form – of something whose content is already present [prior to this thought] [...] In other words, philosophy proper is

excluded, but its content continues to be taught, albeit in an improperly philosophical form, in a nonphilosophical manner [...] This schema, so familiar by now, is one of the principal targets of the GREPH'. Derrida, 'The Age of Hegel', pp.31–32.

[33] Derrida, 'The Age of Hegel', p.33.

[34] Virginia Woolf, *To the Lighthouse* (London: Triad/Grafton Books, 1977), pp.40–1.

[35] Jacques Derrida, 'The Principle of Reason: The University in the Eyes of its Pupils', *Diacritics* 13:3 (1983), p.5.

[36] Derrida, 'The Principle of Reason', p.10.

[37] Derrida, 'The Principle of Reason', p.17.

Simon Morgan Wortham is Principal Lecturer in English Literature at the University of Portsmouth and the author of *Rethinking the University: Leverage and Deconstruction* (Manchester University Press, 1999) and *Samuel Weber: Acts of Reading* (Ashgate, 2003). He is currently editing a collection of essays on deconstruction and technology and writing a new book on obscssion.

parallax, 2004, vol. 10, no. 2, 19–36

Audit Society, Practical Deconstruction and Strategic Public Relations

Jeremy Valentine

> *It's not rocket science, nor do the laws of plagiarism apply to ideas.*
> *Look at what other people do, if it works use it, if it doesn't make*
> *sure it is not in your plans.*
> Bob Fenton, Chief Press Officer British Energy, 'To fail
> to plan is to plan to fail', *PR Student*

> *Deconstruction, therefore, borrows its notions, names, or 'concepts'*
> *from philosophy in order to name what is unnameable within*
> *its closure.*
> Rodolphe Gasché, *The Tain of the Mirror*

> *Accentuate the positive, eliminate the negative, and don't mess with*
> *Mister In-Between.*
> Bing Crosby and the Andrews Sisters

Practical, as opposed to what exactly?

In a series of interviews originally published in France in 1993 and subsequently translated, re-edited and published in English in 2002 Derrida addressed the question of the precise nature of the relation between the time of the present and the public sphere.[1] For Derrida these two terms are related by a common 'artifactuality' determined by teletechnology such that actuality, the temporality of the present, is artificial and is made by and on behalf of forces and interests. To illustrate this point Derrida conscientiously refers to the 'artifactual' conditions of his own specific enunciation, to the fact that there is nothing natural and unmediated about the circumstances in which the interviews take place, the bulk of which are filmed. For students and practitioners in media and culture Derrida's observation is hardly news. Indeed, given the ambient scepticism and tactical cynicism which characterizes popular attitudes to 'artifactuality' one might speculate that Derrida is simply expressing a reflexive, tacit taken for granted common sense attitude prevalent within post-modern societies. The aggregate force of such opinions might make an ethical responsibility to '*demonstrate* that the "live" and "real time" are never pure, that they

parallax
ISSN 1353-4645 print/ISSN 1460-700X online © 2004 Taylor & Francis Ltd
http://www.tandf.co.uk/journals
DOI: 10.1080/1353464042000208495

do not give us intuition or transparency, a perception stripped of interpretation or technical intervention'[2] redundant, especially since in many cases artifactuality has given up the pretence of pretending otherwise, for example in its relations with entertainment.

Derrida makes two points against this line of argument. Firstly, to abandon a critical perspective on artifactuality would be to concede that which remains to be proven, and which can be condensed in the notion of an omnipotent and totalizing imperialist system of teletechnology, an ontological order of completion, and which coincides with teletechnology's self-image through which it promotes its advantages. Secondly, Derrida argues against the resigned normalization of 'simulacrum and delusion' precisely in order to affirm the singularity and heterogeneity of artifactuality against the reassuring alibi that it is a space structured and closed by the guarantees of teletechnology. In this respect Derrida anticipates a subsequent critique of immanentism, and thus of the closure of positive or negative ontology.[3] By the same token Derrida also undermines the possibility that one could simply locate and occupy an enunciative position radically exterior to artifactuality, a sovereign power of unmediated presence that would function as a point of opposition by representing itself as a moral and epistemological authority through a privileged relation to *factuality*, and which would mirror all the characteristics of that to which it imagines itself opposed. No one would object to the observation that the regime of artifactuality is not dialogic. But it does not follow from this that the regime is effective in a direct causal manner everywhere and at all times, notwithstanding the thesis of *The Matrix*.

Under these circumstances the durable metaphysical oppositions between philosophy and rhetoric cease to organize a critical force. Instead, to indicate a strategy of critical comportment Derrida refers to and affirms the dissenting force of the untimeliness of the time of the present and the precipitation of *différance*, of the event. The event frustrates the closure of artifactuality. We might say that the value of the event derives from its function as the name for the impossible yet necessary relation between an orientation to the future and an experience of a future in the present, and which thus displaces the punctuality of the present. The relation is impossible because if a future is known, however minimally, then it will not be and is no longer a future. The relation is necessary in the absence of a point in time and space from which everything can be known. As the saying goes: 'time is what prevents everything happening at once'. Thus the event is neither accidental nor contingent and cannot be subsumed within a speculative teleology or empiricist calculus of probability. It is the gap between orientation and experience. It could be a good thing or a bad thing but it is not fatal.[4]

In Derrida's work this approach to the event partly derives from the critique of the temporalization of auto-affection in Husserl's phenomenology.[5] Elsewhere in Derrida's work the logic of the event has been addressed through an interrogation of the thematics of messianicity.[6] Messianicity is the experience of the anticipation of a messiah before any actual messiah emerges from the future to occupy this position. On the one hand we might say that the event is the privileged object of deconstruction, the movement of taking-place. Yet on the other the event is always *an* event, *this* event. The event of teletechnological artifactuality is linked to a movement of deconstruction which Derrida scopes in the following terms:

What the accelerated development of teletechnologies, of cyberspace, of the new topology of 'the virtual' is producing is a practical *deconstruction* of the traditional and dominant concepts of the state and citizen (and thus of 'the political') as they are linked to the actuality of a territory. I say 'deconstruction' because, ultimately, what I name and try to think under this word is, at bottom, nothing other than this very process, its 'taking-place' in such a way that its happening affects the very experience of place, and the recording (symptomatic, scientific, or philosophical) of this 'thing', the trace that traces (inscribes, preserves, carries, refers, or defers) the différance of this event which happens to place [*qui arrive au lieu*] – which happens to take place, and to taking-place [*qui arrive à (l') avoir-lieu*] [...].[7]

Although we may suspect a degree of technological determinism in Derrida's observation, which is perhaps over generous in acknowledging the methodological requirement to preserve the phenomenal forms of appearances, it is the notion and scope of 'practical deconstruction' that can be operationalized for the analysis of the political dynamic of contemporary regimes of signification understood in terms of the dominance of artifactuality. That is to say, for an analysis of 'practical deconstruction' and not the deconstruction of contemporary regimes of signification, as if deconstruction could be attributed to the action or intention of a subject or agent, for example as a methodology.

The relation between practical deconstruction and artifactuality can be indicated by reference to two further quotations from Derrida which, removed from their context of enunciation and interlocution, frame the quotation by a matter of minutes. So, before:

> Right, every right, in a certain sense, is a right of inspection, every right gives the right of inspection. Right equals 'right of inspection'. Kant reminded us of this, that there is no right without the ability to exercise the force that will ensure it is respected. Thus there is no right that does not consist in conferring upon a power a right to control and surveillance and, therefore, a right of inspection, in a situation where nothing guarantees it 'naturally'.[8]

And then, after:

> As always, the choice is not *between* mastery and nonmastery, any more than it is *between* writing and nonwriting in the everyday sense. The way in which I had tried to define writing implied that it was already, as you [Bernard Stiegler, J.V.] noted, a teletechnology, with all that this entails of an original expropriation. The choice does not choose between control and noncontrol, mastery and nonmastery, property or expropriation. What is at stake here, and it obeys another 'logic', is rather a 'choice' between multiple configurations of mastery without mastery (what I have proposed to call '*exappropriation*'). But it also takes the phenomenal form of a war, a conflictual tension between multiple

strategies of control. Even if no one can ever control everything, it is a question of knowing whom you want to restrict, by what and by whom you don't want what you say or what you do to be immediately and totally reappropriated. I'm not under any illusion about the possibility of my controlling or appropriating what I do, what I say or what I am, but I do want – this is the point of every struggle, of every drive in this domain – I would at least like the things I say and do not to be immediately and clearly used towards ends I feel I must oppose. I don't want to reappropriate my product, but for the same reason, I don't want others doing this towards ends I feel I must fight. It's a struggle, really, between multiple movements of appropriation, or of exappropriation, an illusionless struggle precisely because it gets displaced between two equally inaccessible poles.[9]

Derrida locates political activity in terms of its dislocation and displacement which is traced within an economy of signification which cannot be contained for the very reason that its exappropriation is its source of value or surplus. Exappropriation is both condition and stake in relations of mastery and non-mastery. Derrida's position is purely political in the sense that it has abandoned the alibi of ideology in both its positive and negative senses, either as the expression or legitimation of an interest, or as a structure of illusion or dissembling. Rather, the political is conceived as a relation between the means of demonstrating the exercise of a right and the movement or forces through which a right is displaced. It is within this relation that the event takes place precisely because exappropriation is both the condition and limit of artifactuality or, in the idiom of the analysis of deconstruction, its simultaneous possibility and impossibility. It is the relation between the exercise of a right of signification and the verification of this right which cannot be determined. Teletechnology both affirms the right and displaces the means of its verification. Artifactuality is not exterior to this relation.

The purpose of this paper is to locate the taking-place of practical deconstruction within a teletechnological regime of artifactuality by focussing on the relation between the exercise of a right of signification and its verification. To do that the paper will examine the case of audit as a teletechnology of verification and its place within the UK Public Relations business in the process of attempting to hegemonize the field of artifactuality itself. That is to say, the Public Relations business in the UK anticipates a messianistic event in which it will delegate to itself the power to organize, institutionalize and audit a regime of artifactuality in order to verify that the regime is artifactual, and thus to confirm its place within it. As we shall see, this has everything to do with the relation between audit and its conditions, and with the fact that for audit to take place these conditions are non-auditable. At stake in audit is the means of accounting for the exercise of 'rights of inspection' in that audit is a teletechnology designed for the displacement of such means. Audit artifactualizes the accounts. So the political question concerns the identification of relations of mastery and non-mastery within the teletechnological forms through which this takes place. Hopefully doing so will help to shed further light on the practical relation between deconstruction and the political that Derrida alludes to in the above quotation. To do this we must trace the event of audit itself.

The event of audit

Audit is a teletechnology designed to objectify that which is not organized within spaces of actions, and thus to contribute to the further organization of actions. By making actions auditable they become organizable. According to Power's concise and forensic account[10] this is done by making organizational systems and processes and those subjects which are attributed to the actions through which they take place 'auditable' by interpreting and representing qualitative performances as quantifiable measures. In this respect audit establishes a regime of artifactuality. 'Organizations must be changed to make them auditable'[11] such that 'when organizations do not have clear measures of productivity which relate their inputs to their outputs, the *audit* of efficiency and effectiveness is in fact a process of *defining* and operationalizing measures of performance for the audited entity. In short the efficiency and effectiveness of organizations is not so much verified as constructed around the audit process itself'.[12] Hence the purpose of auditing is to establish a representation which causes a subjective experience of 'confidence'.

In this way 'audit' responds to the decline of 'trust in trust' which for Power constitutes a widespread social phenomenon. Although audit seeks to establish compliance between systems, actions and their meanings, for example through the construction of 'aims, objectives and outcomes' as authoritative measures, compliance is never enough as it may simply be an effect of audit and not of the actual relations between systems, actions and meanings. As auditees become subjected to audit they learn its requirements and so adapt to meet them. Thus: 'Assumptions of distrust sustaining audit processes may be self-fulfilling as auditees adapt their behaviour strategically in response to the audit process, thereby becoming less trustworthy'.[13] In such circumstances audit simply audits the effects of itself and thus invents more things to audit in order to have work to do. Not surprisingly the symptom of audit as a technology of representations is an adversarial environment of blame allocation and risk displacement and competition between and innovation within the performance of impression and reputation management. Thus; 'in allocating problems to auditing institutions not only are the boundaries between instrumental assurance and policy evaluation constantly breached but audit and inspection are also seen to constitute the conduct of politics by other means, a characteristic they share with war'.[14] Power provides an excellent historical analogy for the situation. Thus:

> In this respect one might compare this imperative with that which informed the detailed output targets of the former Soviet Union. This was a situation characterised by pathologies of 'creative compliance' [...], poor quality goods and the development of survival skills to show that, often impossible, targets were achieved. Games are played around an 'indicator' culture where auditable performance is an end in itself and real long term planning is impossible.[15]

The absence of trust in and knowledge of organizations and systems is sublimated by the displacement of trust onto the process of audit through which organizations and systems are represented as knowable.

However, what is peculiar about audit is that it is itself designed to be resistant to objectification. Audit verifies what it creates but audit itself is not verifiable. There is no independent verification of audit as the criteria for its measure would have to be that it is not auditable. Circulating as a commodity in 'inscrutable markets' the 'essential obscurity of the audit product is offset by massive investment in formal procedural audit knowledge and in the development of professional codes of ethics, rules of independence and so on'.[16] The success of audit can only ever be established in terms of the fact that audit has taken place and so failure, in the sense of an obstacle to audit, is simply the precipitation of more audit such that audit valorises the value which audit adds; 'audit has put itself beyond empirical knowledge about its own effects in favour of a constant programmatic affirmation of its potential'.[17] So audit produces itself, or more audit. Thus: 'The abstract system tends to become the primary external auditable object, rather than the output of the organization itself, and this adds to the obscurity of the audit as a process which provides assurance about systems elements and little else'.[18] Hence the secret of audit. It must be;

> 'practical' enough to look like guidance to outsiders but not so practical that these outsiders could replicate or judge it without the help of insiders. In this way disturbances to the system, in the form of new demands, or old demands with a new rhetoric, can be managed by transforming the unfamiliar and intractable into the familiar and possible.[19]

The indeterminacy of audit is not just a resource for self-valorisation. It is also a resource through which relations of exchange are established by exploiting any agenda, strategy or practice which can be identified as a source of profit. These are relations of power, of mastery and non-mastery, and as such should be understood within a political logic which allows audit to expand its jurisdiction both within and across organizations.

Power describes this logic as a 'reverse effect', and which operates in two complimentary ways. Firstly, 'decoupling', the creation of agencies within an organization tasked with managing the auditing process and making the organization auditable. These agencies advance their own agendas within the organization in order to benefit from resource allocation through promoting distrust and undermining confidence by drawing attention to the absence of objectivity. As a consequence, organizational activities become consumed by the infinite task of representing in an auditable way the structures and systems and processes which are supposed to make organizational activities possible. Auditing is the cure for the disease it creates. The circle is not entirely closed however as the organizational autonomy which the objectivity of audit aims to weaken, or 'professional capture', is replaced by the autonomization of the audit process itself. Audit becomes the profession that captures the organization. This gives rise to the second consequence, 'colonization', the creation of a new organizational actor which aims to challenge the power of an organization by subjecting its activities to the technology of audit. This works because the technology of audit is promoted as a benefit to the organization which will deliver measurable improvements, but which are in reality only the appearance that the organization has become auditable, and thus repair the damage to trust and confidence which audit has caused.[20] Hence the action of the organization becomes orientated to the requirement that it is auditable, and thus that it should appear *to itself* to be less heterogeneous, less complex, less uncertain. In this way it will be encouraged to understand itself as the subject of absolute knowledge in which existence is revealed in full transparency.

One could say that Power's account of the 'audit society' suggests that audit is practical deconstruction in the terms laid out above in and through the taking place or event of audit, and which Power captures through the notions of 'auditing and the dialectic of failure' and 'the essential obscurity of auditing', and which is expressed positively as the 'expectations gap'.[21] That is to say, a gap between what audit promises, or the 'programmatic' or moral dimension of audit, the ends of audit, and the means to deliver this promise, the 'technological' or implementation dimension of audit. The event of audit takes place precisely as this 'expectations gap' and is sustained by it. Audit will take place, but the effects of audit are not accountable. Hence more audit fills the gap. Or, to be more precise, audit takes place on the condition that it will not have taken place in order to take place again. Thus, without an expectations gap 'there would be full transparency of the audit process, both in terms of its objectives and its production of assurance in relation to those objectives'.[22] The key to its success is the very indeterminacy of audit itself from which arises the gap between its normative force and the means of its implementation. The gap stimulates expectations which cannot be met except through the application of more auditing. Audit is messianistic.

Yet the location of deconstruction is something which is added on to Power's account, at its limit. Although Power's text is exemplary and adds greatly to our understanding of the phenomenon, primarily by constituting audit as an object, the limit of the account becomes visible with respect to the very indeterminacy of the object itself. On the one hand Power shows very clearly how audit positivizes its own indeterminacy, yet on the other Power does not account for how this indeterminacy takes place, or what we might understand in a very approximate or preliminary way as its conditions. We can see this limit with respect to the conditions of audit which Power does identify. For Power these are located in terms of the distinction between agency and structure, although Power is careful not to turn this into a paradigmatic opposition. On the one hand audit works because those subject to it see it as in their interest to comply. Hence audit works as a consequence of 'rational choice' in which agents seek and accumulate positional advantages. On the other hand audit works because it embeds in the structure of the organization occupied by those subject to it. Hence audit works as a consequence of a conservative disposition to comply with 'how things are' for fear of the adverse consequences, and because compliance requires less effort than opposition. Agents thus strategically refuse or simply lack knowledge with which to undermine audit, and which thus increases their exposure to auditing. Hence agency, structure and audit converge in the following way: 'The problem of the epistemological obscurity of audit means that it is difficult to disentangle instrumental effects from a certain staging of control; audit practice is a form of social control talk'.[23]

Without doubt both agency and structure are essential explanatory frameworks, and the reality is probably at various points along the scale between them depending on particular circumstances. Yet they only explain compliance, or at least its appearance. They do not explain the force of the 'expectations gap', the agency of the 'epistemological obscurity' of audit, only the poles of its relations. In other words they do not explain the conditions of the gap. Despite Power's nuances, audit is reduced to an opposition between agency and structure in which each term attempts to occupy the ground of the other, and in doing so the distinction between the two terms evaporates. Agency is a form of structure in that it is predictable and regular, structure is a form of agency in that it acts and is acted upon. If this opposition exhausts the field of possibilities then audit is guaranteed as if it does not take place it will take place, at some future point. Audit's telos becomes verified as the ground of its explanation. In which case the 'expectations gap' does not take place except as a pre-determined effect and the indeterminacy of audit dissolves. There is no longer the possibility that audit will or will not take place, and thus of relations of exappropriation and mastery and non-mastery which structure this possibility, and thus politics. Therefore, in order to think this possibility we should consider the question of the possibility of accounting for the effects of auditing which audit cannot account for itself, or represent to itself as the condition of representing itself to others within the regime of representation or artifactuality which audit seeks to establish, or what Power calls the 'reverse effect'. And to do that we shall have to go beyond the evidence provided by Power's text, both to confirm and displace it.

Exorbitant accounting

According to Power auditing derives from the institutions of financial accounting. Historically, one of the events which precipitated the rise of auditing was the series of spectacular financial scandals and frauds which emerged as part of post-modernizing processes in the 1980s – and which continue up to now and beyond. This was never a case of capitalism suddenly becoming venal and corrupt. Rather, bearers of capital simply discovered ways to out-manoeuvre representational techniques of financial objectivity and these activities became visible within a destabilizing context of mergers, acquisitions and vertical and horizontal disintegration. Ironically, auditing was developed as a fee based service provided by those same firms which had developed systems of financial accounting as a non-financial but pseudo quantifiable strategy for representing the systems and processes through which finances flowed in such a way as to suggest that any misappropriation was purely accidental. One might add that financial accounting firms developed auditing in order to create new markets for their services, which had been hit by the increased use of computers and accountancy packages in organizations, and therefore the phenomenon can be placed within the general growth of management consulting.

Although such events are predictable and unremarkable, and thus not really events at all, the relation between auditing and accounting contains the possibility of accounting for a form of accounting which could account for what cannot be accounted for within the form of accounting which audit seeks to establish. That is to say, a non-instrumental form of accounting, or, to say the same thing differently, an account of deconstruction which would account for the event of deconstruction within accounting itself. To think such a possibility we can observe that despite its hegemonic status financial accounting is one particular form of accounting in which an equivalence between the real world and a restricted economy is secured. Needless to say this labour of equivalence remains unaccounted for in both financial accounting and the forms of audit through which it is translated. It is a cost which cannot be priced and thus relies on and trusts in a prior moment or *mise en scene* which cannot be accounted for and within the system of representation which accounting desires to organize and the grounds through which such a system is secured.[24]

To show the implication of deconstruction within and for accounting we can refer to an account of deconstruction which would establish its methodological consequences in order to show that the difference between system and ground is internal to the larger hegemony of metaphysics, of the hegemonic form of hegemony, to which financial accounting is subordinate. Here we refer to Gasché's demonstration of the necessary failure of any attempt to establish deconstruction as an object subordinate to the instrumental requirements of a subject who would be secured by the mastery of method.[25] To account for deconstruction is an 'exorbitant' endeavour.[26] It is this failure which distinguishes deconstruction from any notion of a strategy which reveals logical contradiction or argumentative fallacy or inconsistency. Rather, an account of deconstruction is an account of the systematic and regulated nature of contradiction, argumentation and inconsistency through which coherency, totality and clarity are produced. 'Deconstruction is thus the attempt to account for the heterogeneity constitutive of the philosophical discourse, not by trying to overcome its inner differences but by maintaining them'.[27] In other words deconstruction cannot be explained away by reference to or dissolved within a ground or essence or synonym thereof. This might suggest that deconstruction could be substituted for a place radically exterior from and opposed to accounting. On the contrary, deconstruction takes place within accounting and understands the heterogeneity in terms of infrastructures, 'the *formal rule* that each time regulates differently the play of the contradictions in question'[28] to which accounting is subordinate. That is to say, infrastructures account for the methods through which heterogeneity is maintained, the justifications and demonstrations with respect to grounds, reasons or causes through which accounting takes place.

Although we may hold reservations about Gasché's account of infrastructure, which, at best positivizes the limits of Derrida's own account of deconstruction – '*Structure*, as used by Derrida, is an infrastructure'[29] – simply because this account is not exterior to metaphysics and its infrastructures, and thus opens up the infrastructurality within both Gasché's and Derrida's account of deconstruction – 'it is, rigorously speaking, improper to refer to infrastructures *as such*'[30] because there is 'no *as such* to the infrastructures'[31] – nevertheless Gasché provides a convincing account of the operational logic of infrastructures. Infrastructures are not of the order of being or non-being or of opposition as such but account for the putting into place of such oppositions. They do so by linking 'all the threads of correspondence among certain heterogeneous *points of presence* within a discourse or text'[32] and are thus proximate to concepts of overdetermination, articulation and mediation. Infrastructures are neither a ground nor that which may be shown to rest upon it but the difference between these two moments of accounting, their simultaneous and equivocal conditions of possibility and impossibility, or play. In this respect infrastructures are radically contextualizing in that they inscribe the trace of possibilities subsequently structured as an origin, and thus unground an origin, centre, or telos. 'An origin presupposes this play as a text presupposes its context, a book its margins, a painting its frame, or any unity its border'.[33] In other words, infrastructures inscribe relations of mastery and non-mastery, the possibility of exappropriation.

Thus infrastructures are a form of accounting for that which cannot be accounted for within established systems of accounting. 'The economy of the infrastructures takes into account that which exceeds accounting, that which, as a result, is never repaid in accounting'.[34] Infrastructures account but necessarily and by definition cannot be accounted for. 'It is impossible to account for something that inscribes the operation of accounting in a cluster of structural possibilities that exclude their own self-domination and self-reflection'.[35] There is no exteriority of accounting, there are only determinate and contingent limits which are internal to the operation of accounting itself, and of which accounting cannot account. Therefore, in no sense is the interior relation of accounting and deconstruction a matter of crossing the line. On the contrary, the outside of accounting is produced from within accounting itself, and which is not itself an outside with regard to an inside, but only the moment of the displacement of its limit or closure. For this reason the values of transgression and excess are inherently narcissistic. And in those popular cases where this displacement is represented as an opposition then the antagonism is purely an internal affair. Thus: 'For this reason it is incorrect to speak of a transgression or excess at all'.[36] There is only a determined surplus, or infrastructure.

Mastery and non-mastery in the UK Public Relations business

Within audit the hegemonic form of accounting is ungrounded, subordinated to the difference between the system of representation and the ground represented from within it, by the diversion of costs from the core activities of the organization to the technology of its audit which verifies these core activities simply by the judgement that they are auditable. The price of the judgement is calculated on the basis of the core activities to which the judgement does not contribute, and the cost is absorbed by the audited organization, often by reducing costs elsewhere. Within Power's account this corresponds to the logic of the 'reverse effect' which enables the play of exappropriation and relations of mastery and non-mastery which sustain the 'expectations gap', or the infrastructure of accounting. It is thus the condition of the expansion of both the hegemonic form of accounting and its audit derivative, or 'de-coupling' and 'colonization', and thus of the 'expectations gap', beyond an origin. In this respect auditing is internal to the scope of the 'practical deconstruction' of the political. The banality of 'practical deconstruction' can be shown by examining the relations between mastery and non-mastery within a domain which is both subject to audit and at the same time the subject of audit in its attempts to inscribe 'reverse effects'. Like audit, Public Relations (PR) is an 'inscrutable market'. In part this inscrutability is deliberate in order to protect the 'expertise' which PR claims to possess from price competition, but the inscrutability is itself the verification of the expertise which PR claims in the form of 'reputation management'.

Public Relations might seem a rather dull and banal example to consider. If so then the choice is deliberate as it will serve to make a criticism of Derrida's account of the political which is that the force and power of banality is not comprehended by the 'heroic' modes of the modern political imaginary to which Derrida refers. Derrida's remarks on the political are limited by a focus on the negative effects of 'practical deconstruction' on the Schmittian form of the political and its historical antagonist, liberalism.[37] This serves to obscure the event of the political itself in the sense of the unanticipated consequences of the displacement of the logic of mastery and non-mastery. That is to say, the infrastructure of the political itself. Indeed, 'practical deconstruction' is possibly co-extensive with any domain subject to the structural transformations and dedifferentiation of post-modernization. Here we can refer to such phenomena as the transformation of the links between strategies of capital accumulation and the political structures through which they are regulated, in Western Europe at least, which are expressed as the creation of markets in rents and the dissolution of the authority structures of government within games of governance.[38] These games typically take the form of mimicking commercial practices in state-government-citizen relations, and are variously referred to as the 'regulatory state', the 'hollowed-out state' or 'New Public Management', in which pseudo-market relations are institutionalized in the form of the 'principal-agent' or 'purchaser-provider split'.[39]

Moreover, as well as introducing economic questions of efficiency into the political the distribution of authority and control is itself subject to the same displacements, which requires the invention of rules of translation through which the qualitative becomes quantifiable and measurable. This expansion into the sphere of the political is at the same time an expansion of the political beyond the institutional spaces in which it had previously been confined, albeit without the forms of accountability which had been developed to legitimate the exercise of political power. Perhaps Deleuze captured this process and anticipated many of its forms in his essay on the replacement of disciplinary society with 'societies of control'.[40] In his comments on Deleuze, Hardt observes how these phenomena point to the collapse of the distinction between state and civil society, and to the 'real subsumption' of labour in capital.[41] Yet it is Deleuze's description of the causality of these phenomena in terms of the 'undulations of the snake' which most accurately captures the logic of 'practical deconstruction'. It is through a snake-like movement of de-coupling and colonization that Public Relations enters into this terrain.

Using data from ethnographic participant observation training sessions in PR and entries to the annual 'Sword of Excellence' (yes, really) competition run by the Institute of Public Relations (IPR), Pieczka has produced a detailed Bourdieusian description of the 'logic of practice' of PR expertise in which 'decoupling' and 'colonization' have become increasingly reflective.[42] Pieczka demonstrates that PR is organized as a response to the 'practical deconstruction' of the political. Thus the PR habitus is centred on a 'picture of the world' in which;

> power in society is moving away from its traditional centres in government and business and spreading over a wider social base; national boundaries are reconfigured as regional and global at the same time; legitimacy is defined from the narrow understanding of what is legal and increasingly in terms of what is moral; citizenship is expressed through consumerism, and all this is fuelled by the technological

changes in communication and the resulting changes in the mass media.[43]

For PR this situation also provides an opportunity for intervention, and thus its own valorisation. According to PR, as old certainties and controls disappear they are replaced by a reduction of action to uniform political, civil and economic institutions, and aspirations to narrowly understood notions of prosperity. Publics are characterized in terms of increased pessimism, criticism and suspicion. In other words, the scope of 'practical deconstruction' is treated as positive knowledge within PR and which enjoys the status of risk through which relations of mastery and non-mastery are calibrated. In this context the role of PR is to make its clients legitimate by instrumentalizing moral concerns and reinterpreting or re-naming the forces which constitute the context in which clients act. The difficulty PR faces derives from the refusal of agents to get locked into fixed relationships within a 'permanently fractured world, unpredictable, driven by emotion, and spinning on forever new issues'.[44] PR takes advantage of this context by claiming to provide solutions for clients who find themselves subject to it by representing itself as a space of linear causality in which the internal relations of a client organization, its external surface appearance or 'corporate self', and the environment which threatens and sustains it are co-ordinated. These solutions are essentially cultural in that they aim to articulate the symbolic and the material against the real, the environment of unmasterable fragmentation. Hence a solution would typically take the form of the abolition of the distinction between perception and reality in order to manipulate perception and thus change reality.[45]

The problem with PR's pragmatic artifactuality is not epistemological but political. It concerns the location of the perceiving subject; is it the client, the public, or the PR agent itself, demonstrating to itself its own success? The question can only be verified negatively through the re-emergence of the real and the dislocation of the symbolic and material fit. The possibility of dislocating the material-symbolic fit within PR arises from two sources. Firstly, rival businesses which can provide similar services such as advertising, marketing and management consultancy. Secondly, the dynamics of popular culture which seek to avoid relationships which lock it into regimes of signification, into a symbolic-material hegemonic fit. If we consider a recent account of the economic value of PR and the status of its business practices which was produced in conjunction with the UK Government we can see both the collapse of the material-symbolic fit within the PR agent itself, and the expression of its desire to establish a series of 'reverse effects' through which it hopes to overcome its abject state.

In November 2003 the Institute of Public Relations (IPR) published a report *Unlocking the Potential of Public Relations: Developing Good Practice*.[46] The report was co-funded by the UK Department of Trade and Industry (DTI) and the research was carried out by the European Centre *for* Business Excellence. It is comprised of interpretations of the statistical analysis of an opinion poll of and summaries of focus groups with workers in the PR business. The publication was accompanied by a report overview *Unlock Your Potential: Key Factors for PR Success* from Michael Murphy, CEO of a PR firm called 'hatch-group' who had chaired the steering group behind the report, a further set of Steering Group Recommendations, a Summary of Findings, a Project Overview, and a foreword from Michael Murphy.

Each of these texts (available from google) is a series of interpretations yet the relations between them do not constitute a closed, homogeneous space of commensurability. The main report is self-described as a 'snapshot of a rolling wave' in order to crudely combine the truth-value of photography with an unstoppable and unpredictable force of nature 'going forward' into an unknown future, yet its contents provide evidence for more static phenomena. In fact the DTI-IPR report inscribes the status of its own agency within itself in terms of its own account of the production line through which PR is produced, which goes from research and analysis, planning, resourcing, doing and measuring. The text corresponds to the first two moments of this process as an attempt to 'simplify the complex' and 'sell benefits and gain agreement'.[47] It does not succeed in this endeavour despite its attempt to present itself through the simplistic and stylized forms of graphs, bullet-points and an intellectually bankrupt state-subsidized positivism. It is within the space between the text's representation of its intentions and its networks of interpretations which attempt to stabilize them that the 'expectations gap' between aims and objectives, programmes and technology, morality and action, which sustains the PR business becomes visible. That is to say, the infrastructure of the report evidences the practical deconstruction of the regime of artifactuality which PR would establish, and in respect to which it identifies its own agency. The evidence takes the form of a crisis which the report describes at the financial, epistemological, organizational and semiotic levels, and which is caused by the conditions which make PR viable. The crisis concerns the collapse of the artifactuality of PR itself and of the teletechnologies through which these are inscribed and verified, and thus of the ability of PR to sustain the messianism of its 'expectations gap'.

This is immediately apparent if the texts are read in the order in which they are presented. Murphy's foreword affirms that 'maintaining and improving the UK's competitive position demands an ethical, dynamic and strategic public relations industry' but also that 'the already significant contribution of the public relations industry to the UK economy can be greatly increased through better understanding by business leaders about what the best of public relations can achieve'. The latter statement would, if implemented, certainly increase PR's share of the UK economy by creating a demand for it but it does not follow that the growth or competitiveness of the UK economy would improve, assuming that it is possible to objectify the referent. Indeed the main report notes that the PR business is currently characterized by a decline in fee income and a plateau in market growth,[48] with quantification proving to be 'problematic'. Despite the optimism expressed by the survey the business has entered 'a period of consolidation and slower growth'.[49] More significantly, the findings 'underline the difficulties of defining clearly the boundaries of what PR is and what the industry covers'.[50] That is, if the business does not know what it is, then it would be difficult to measure its contribution to a national economy, whatever conventions one used for doing so.

There are two sides to this crisis within PR. The first concerns the subjectivity of PR agency. With respect to the statistical analysis of the quality of PR workers the report states that: 'Most respondents rate their organizations highly in terms of their ability to recruit competent PR professionals suggesting that this is not a major issue in the industry'.[51] Yet the summary of findings reports 'a need for real progress in education and training across the public relations industry' and the focus group analysis reports that a 'future trend' will be that: 'Public misconceptions of PR will lead to problems in recruiting the right people', and which, perhaps unfortunately, immediately follows the statement that: 'Recruitment into PR will be increasingly dominated by women'.[52] This problem needs to be addressed in order to enable the fulfilment of PR's aspiration to become a 'management discipline' which would exercise 'high level thought leadership' and satisfy its narcissistic craving to be 'treated as a professional partner rather than as a supplier', i.e. as equivalent to legal and accountancy professionals and not as a trade, and thus overcome its negative self-image and sublimate feelings of insecurity.[53] These problems probably explain the rapid PR personnel turnover, with most employees lasting only 2–3 years, and where: 'Managing 24/7 global communications has a negative impact on quality of life for PR staff'.

The crisis is most vocal in the bullet-pointing of the key points of the focus groups. On the one hand these affirm the desired effects of PR.[54] PR personnel *should* be the 'conscience of the company' integral to 'corporate strategy' by taking a longer-term view from 'inside the top management team' and creating a 'seamless' relationship between 'the perception and reality of an organisation'. Otherwise 'top-down strategies developed as part of a corporate strategy-making process can be problematic without specialist PR input' and clients should be encouraged to 'share future plans'. In fact all personnel are working on PR because they represent the organization. The public itself is also employed in a PR capacity where it learns to understand the benefits of PR. In other words, PR desires a robust, structured system of support so that it can be flexible and fluid, 'involved in implementation on a day-to-day basis'. Thus 'Having efficient administrative processes, therefore, can serve to create the freedom to be creative'.[55] The world has to be fixed, stable and structured so that PR can be mobile, fluid and contingent. The world has to be mastered so that PR can be non-mastered.

The second aspect concerns PR's failure to establish relations which secure a seamless material-symbolic fit between perception and reality. This is imposed by the problem of demonstrating the benefits and advantages of PR. 'Good PR evaluation measures what is important rather than what is easy to measure. It is easier to measure PR outputs (such as coverage) rather than outcomes (such as changing public attitudes)'. This is good PR from the perspective of PR and not of its client. Yet because the 'impact of PR is often indirect' it follows that 'cause and effect cannot be proven'. Pragmatically; 'Good PR evaluation does not waste resources seeking to quantify the unquantifiable but instead uses simple subjective measures of creativity, quality of work and the main outcomes in these more difficult areas'. Hence it is the appearance of PR itself that demonstrates its value. Moreover, an 'over-rigid evaluation framework may lead to opportunities being missed because they appear not to fit the measurement criteria'. These views are echoed by a series of bullet-pointed complaints which refer to the difficulty PR personnel experience in convincing clients of the benefits of PR, or even the inability of the PR sector to distinguish between good and bad PR. These difficulties are displaced onto criticisms of the clients, but also onto the means of the wider distribution of PR, the media which 'prevents organisations from having their views heard without re-interpretation',[56] and the public itself which holds a 'negative' perception of PR and does not regard it as professional, a problem exacerbated by the increasingly diverse and fragmented nature of a resistant public. Even relations between organizational and independent PR lack trust and PR remains engaged in defensive turf wars with advertising and marketing, thus preventing the 'integration of communication' which each desire, provided that each is at the top of the pile, and where all are subjected to managerial regimes of process efficiency, i.e. audit.

Conclusion: The Political Infrastructure of UK PR

For the DTI-IPR the solution to this crisis is to establish a series of 'reverse effects' which will address the problem of clients who are described as 'lukewarm' in providing the support which PR business feel that they require from them, 'depending on consultancies to do the work' while clients prioritized other activities and failed to fulfil PR's expectations of them.[57] Clients are accused of lacking experience in making PR strategy and lack the necessary interpersonal aspects such as 'human chemistry, openness, communication, dialogue, listening and respect'. Oddly, although clients were not surveyed the report claims to have received statements from clients outlining what they 'need to do to improve either their use of PR agencies/consultancies or their interactions with clients'. These are: 'more involvement in strategy development and briefing; an increased role for in house practitioners in evaluation and selection of agencies/consultancies, including assignment of preferred supplier status; budgetary control over billable hours, fuller utilisation and greater results focus; job swaps between organisations and agencies/consultancies'.[58] In fact, everything PR businesses could wish for.

The solution, which will expand the jurisdiction of the 'expectations gap', is that PR agents within organizations will out-source PR work to independent PR consultancies. In house PR agents will then be able to evaluate and demonstrate the need for and benefits of PR to the organization. PR will be able to define what successful PR is. This strategy of decoupling and colonization follows the logic of audit and builds on the example of management consultancies. Because the benefits of PR cannot be demonstrated to the client then the client has to be re-educated in order to be able to see them. The easiest way to do this is if the client becomes part of the PR business. A similar strategy has been adopted by advertising agencies in the face of scepticism from clients about the effectiveness of their campaigns, with agency partners becoming board members.[59] Perhaps the best example of best practice to copy is the case of the emergence of Human Resources as a dominant force in organizations at the start of the post-industrializing process in the 1970s, where re-named Personnel Departments were able to undermine the power of Finance and Payrolls. However, rather than the private sector the way forward for PR is identified as the public sector, in so far as the distinction can be maintained, and the de-structuring processes of UK Government. Hence PR requires a political solution to is own economic and semiotic problems. Or, to use the phrase of a key PR theorist, the business requires the support and sponsorship of political authority in order to establish a 'dominant coalition'.[60]

The action of PR depends on its ability to maintain its subjective sense of agency which can only be done by avoiding becoming 'locked in' to conventional notions of logic, consistency, and the sorts of relationships of trust which elsewhere PR offers to establish with publics on behalf of its clients. Thus: 'Good PR strategy making provides the means for changing PR messages in an instant, often within hours, according to changing circumstances'.[61] This includes messages about itself. Hence the positive aspect of heterogeneity enables the tactical value of the report through which interpretations can be changed to fit contingent circumstances, and which provide the space for articulating 'reverse effects' with UK government. Thus the report's recommendations 'welcome the Government's acceptance of the Phillis Review of Government Communications Interim recommendations'.[62] Published on 27th August 2003 the Phillis Review (available from google) proposed the creation of the civil service post of Permanent Secretary, Government Communications to audit communication activities in UK Government Departments in order to enhance the work of the National Audit Office and to report to the Public Administration Select Committee in the UK Parliament. Yet the DTI-IPR report does not mention this and very little of the report is directly concerned with relations between the PR business and government and politics. So the recommendation is added to the report in order to articulate with an emerging political regime of communication, and which is imagined by the graphic which badges the document's footer right through the text; the DTI logo is linked to the IPR logo by the icons of an eye, an ear and a mouth.

It is hardly surprising that the IPR is so keen to show a positive response to the Phillis Review as, in addition to creating opportunities for auditing and accreditation which it and its members could undertake, the review also recommended that strategic communications should be integrated into policy implementation, that an authoritative culture which accepts and values communication should be created both within Departments and across government, and that this should impact on civil service promotion. These recommendations are offered as solutions to the problem of a significant decline in trust of government information and between government, politicians, the media and the public. Thus the report is the attempt to establish control over a regime of signification that has gone out of control. Hence as well as the possibility of financial expansion the report also offers the possibility of a stabilized regime of signification enforced by political authority. This will assist the PR business to 'improve competitiveness and overall performance'.[63] UK Government 'should' embed PR within its structure and organizations, encourage civil servants to become PR workers and to procure PR from private PR businesses which will be audited and accredited by government in consultation with PR businesses, regulate the PR market in order to embed PR in the economy, for example by conferring 'chartered' status on PR 'guild-style' bodies, such as the IPR, encourage the adoption of PR throughout the public and private sectors as both a component within organizations and as a commodity to purchase. Thus government offers the possibility of stabilizing a regime of artifactuality which will enable PR to act on others. Again, everything which PR could wish for. If anything, this demonstrates the importance of 'networking', with both Government and IPR feet in both camps.[64]

Of course, this depends on the stability of government itself. This is not a question of the conduct of a party or of a politician or the desires of an electorate, but of the 'practical deconstruction' of its organizational logics which makes the 'reverse effect' of a 'dominant coalition' a possibility for PR. Yet for PR to succeed will require its production of the artifactuality of stabilization, a locked in relation between the structures of government, its image, and the perceptions of its stakeholders. Were this to happen then the value of PR would decline. In which case, there is every possibility that PR will become absorbed by a different logic of events which will be precipitated by its attempt to destabilize its own regime of artifactuality. That is to say, to introduce the crisis of practical deconstruction into the coalition itself, to subvert its seamlessness. This will very much depend on the mastery of timing.

Notes

[1] J. Derrida and B. Stiegler, *Echographies of Television*, trans. J. Bajorek (Cambridge: Polity Press, 2002).

[2] Derrida and Stiegler, *Echographies*, p.5 [original emphasis].

[3] J. Derrida, 'Marx and Sons', trans. G.M. Goshgarian, in M. Sprinker [ed] *Ghostly Demarcations: A Symposium on Jacques Derrida's Specters of Marx* (London: Verso, 1999).

[4] A good overview of Derrida's approach to the relation between time and technology is Derrida, 'Nietzsche and the Machine (Interview with Richard Beardsworth)', *Nietzsche Studies* 7 (1994), pp.7–66.

[5] J. Derrida, *Speech and Phenomena and Other Essays on Husserl's Theory of Signs*, trans. D.B. Allison (Evanston: Northwestern University Press, 1973).

[6] J. Derrida, *Specters of Marx: The State of the Debt, the Work of Mourning, & the New International*, trans. P. Kamuf (London: Routledge, 1994).

[7] Derrida and Stiegler, *Echographies*, p.36 [original emphasis].

[8] Derrida and Stiegler, *Echographies*, p.33.

[9] Derrida and Stiegler, *Echographies*, p.37.

[10] M. Power, *The Audit Society: Rituals of Verification* (Oxford: Oxford University Press, 1997).

[11] Power, *The Audit Society*, p.47.

[12] Power, *The Audit Society*, p.51 [original emphasis].

[13] Power, *The Audit Society*, p.135.

[14] Power, *The Audit Society*, p.67.

[15] Power, *The Audit Society*, p.121.

[16] Power, *The Audit Society*, p.30.

[17] Power, *The Audit Society*, p.142.

[18] Power, *The Audit Society*, p.85.

[19] Power, *The Audit Society*, p.25.

[20] Power, *The Audit Society*, pp.95–98.

[21] Power, *The Audit Society*, pp.25–31.

[22] Power, *The Audit Society*, p.31.

[23] Power, *The Audit Society*, p.141.

[24] On the abyssal logic of financial representation, in this case with respect to the epistemology of prices, see D.G. Carlson, 'On the Margins of Microeconomics', in D. Cornell, M. Rosenfeld and D.G. Carlson [eds], *Deconstruction and the Possibility of Justice* (London: Routledge, 1992).

[25] R. Gasché, *The Tain of the Mirror: Derrida and the Philosophy of Reflection* (Cambridge, Mass.: Harvard University Press, 1986).

[26] J. Derrida, *Of Grammatology*, trans. G.C. Spivak (Baltimore: The Johns Hopkins University Press, 1976), pp.157–164.

[27] Gasché, *The Tain of the Mirror*, p.135.

[28] Gasché, *The Tain of the Mirror*, p.142.

[29] Gasché, *The Tain of the Mirror*, p.147.

[30] Gasché, *The Tain of the Mirror*, p.148 [original emphasis].

[31] Gasché, *The Tain of the Mirror*, p.150 [original emphasis].

[32] Gasché, *The Tain of the Mirror*, p.152.

[33] Gasché, *The Tain of the Mirror*, p.160.

[34] Gasché, *The Tain of the Mirror*, p.162.

[35] Gasché, *The Tain of the Mirror*, p.162.

[36] Gasché, *The Tain of the Mirror*, p.170.

[37] Derrida gives further thought to this relation in *Politics of Friendship*, trans. George Collins (London: Verso, 1997).

[38] B. Jessop, 'Capitalism and its future: remarks on regulation, government and governance', *Review of International Political Economy*, 4:3 (1997), pp.561–581.

[39] P. Du Gay, *in praise of bureaucracy* (London: Sage, 2000); J. Newman, *Modernising Governance: New Labour, Policy and Society* (London: Sage, 2001).

[40] G. Deleuze, 'Postscript on Control Societies', in *negotiations* (New York: Columbia University Press, 1995).

[41] M. Hardt, 'The Withering of Civil Society', *Social Text* 14:4 (1995), pp.27–44

[42] M. Pieczka, 'Public relations expertise deconstructed', *Media, Culture and Society*, 24:3 (2002), pp.301–323.

[43] Pieczka, 'Public relations expertise deconstructed', p.304.

[44] Pieczka, 'Public relations expertise deconstructed', p.310.

[45] Pieczka, 'Public relations expertise deconstructed', p.316.

[46] DTI-IPR, *Unlocking the Potential of Public Relations: Developing Good Practice* (London: Institute of Public Relations, 2003). I am grateful to my colleague

Emma Wood for drawing my attention to these texts.

[47] DTI-IPR, *Public Relations*, p.13.
[48] DTI-IPR, *Public Relations*, p.10.
[49] DTI-IPR, *Public Relations*, p.11.
[50] DTI-IPR, *Public Relations*, p.23.
[51] DTI-IPR, *Public Relations*, p.43.
[52] DTI-IPR, *Public Relations*, p.63.
[53] DTI-IPR, *Public Relations*, p.21.
[54] DTI-IPR, *Public Relations*, p.49–62.
[55] DTI-IPR, *Public Relations*, p.55.
[56] DTI-IPR, *Public Relations*, p.59.
[57] DTI-IPR, *Public Relations*, p.35.
[58] DTI-IPR, *Public Relations*, p.36.
[59] S. Nixon, *advertising cultures* (London: Sage, 2003).
[60] J.E. Grunig [ed], *Excellence in Public Relations and Communication Management* (Hillsdale, New Jersey: Lawrence Erlbaum, 1992); M. Dozier [ed], *Manager's Guide to Excellence in Public Relations and Communication Management* (Mahwah, New Jersey: Erlbaum, 1995). I am grateful to my colleague Andy Piasecki for discussions on this matter.
[61] DTI-IPR, *Public Relations*, p.51.
[62] DTI-IPR, *Public Relations*, p.6.
[63] DTI-IPR, *Public Relations*, p.11.
[64] On the impact of postmodernizing processes on the *Yes Minister* shenanigans of UK Government, see C. Hay and D. Richards, 'The Tangled Web of Westminster and Whitehall', *Public Administration*, 78:1 (2000), pp.1–28.

Jeremy Valentine works in media and culture at Queen Margaret University College, Edinburgh. He is currently interested in emerging relations between culture and governance. He is the co-author, with Benjamin Arditi, of *Polemicization: The Contingency of the Commonplace*, and co-editor of the series *Taking On The Political* with Edinburgh and New York University Presses.

parallax, 2004, vol. 10, no. 2, 37–49

Auditing Education: Deconstruction and the Archiving of Knowledge as Curriculum

Peter Pericles Trifonas

For a very long time now, the globalization of postindustrial society has exhibited the tell-tale signs of a need to audit culture. The effort to identify ideals and values as a point of intersubjective assurance and subjective differentiation has exhausted itself in a grudging acceptance of the assimilation of singularity according to the madness of economic reason. Ethics has become mired in a wave of petulant commercialism and brand tribalism nurtured and supported by the media representation of multinational corporations. The difference of culture has been consumed through the symbolic exchange value of signs that are linked to ideologically motivated images of a simulated reality. Bits and bytes of knowledge now travel faster than ever across the virtual boundaries of time and space. The images of data reflected from translucent screens enhances a digital world picture where all information is considered standing reserve for the free use of individuals whose empirical and epistemological identities are enjoined to a web of globally proliferating incorporate bodies. But is information power? Does it engender freedom? No, not really. Freedom is the ontological condition of ethics not epistemology. Information uses the illusion of power without the agency required to make it knowledge. Information is not knowledge. In itself, it will not set you free or empower you without a praxeological component of subjective action. The spatio-temporal disjunction between theory and praxis engenders multiple perspectives on the impossible conditions of knowledge and non-knowledge that need to be reconciled in accordance with information. Ideas need to be put into action to enact the force of power as *knowledge-in-formation*. The nature of episteme within the concept of culture has become redefined in accordance with the incommensurability between repositories of knowledge, and the technologies of archiving information used to secure the structures and conditions of its reproducibility and define the limits of its transmissive potential. It is not simply a coincidence that the question of education has been central to any consideration of what Jean Baudrillard calls 'the violence of the global',[1] its effects on culture, identity and difference. The function of schools and universities has been a key issue in every major election and political campaign where the future of a society or nation is perceived to be at stake in relation to the (in)ability of its citizens to take up the call to compete on the economic battlefront of global competition. The right to education is tied up with the debt and duty owed by the individual to be productive and contribute to the economic well-being and sustenance of the State. The full pecuniary power of knowledge – its exchange value in the marketplace of ideas, goods and services – is necessarily delayed during the process of

parallax
ISSN 1353-4645 print/ISSN 1460-700X online © 2004 Taylor & Francis Ltd
http://www.tandf.co.uk/journals
DOI: 10.1080/1353464042000208503

education at any level because it is *knowledge-in-formation*. Teaching and learning cannot simply reduce knowledge to an instrumental or symbolic value defined in and of itself primarily by economic gain or benefit. That would be unethical; even though, there is always an outside influence that determines the method and purpose of instruction and the deliberate path of *knowledge-in-formation*. At some undisclosed time in the future, however, when the student citizen applies the principles of knowledge in the form of work and labour and begins to take full advantage of public amenities, there is an obligation that must be forfeit to repay the debt and duty owed to the State for draining the availability of the resources supplied. The obligation extends beyond the monetary sphere into the ethical dimension of citizenship as cultural participation. Checks and balances for securing the development of autonomous individuals capable of creative self-actualization and economic self-sufficiency are built into any educational system. But the cultural survival of nations and States depends on more than the ability of its citizens to become employable and productive workers to secure the competitive advantage of a labour force in a global context. Policy does indeed regulate the theoretical and practical ability of educational institutions to achieve precise goals and objectives.

The knowledge structures of science as 'moments of learning' are the minimal parameters of *what we know* that legitimize knowledge as the interest of research. Their institution within the material expression and social trappings of consciousness signals the public degree of their acceptance and forms the relative foundations of *what we think we know* at a basic level of understanding and representation. Fundamental knowledge is not complete in itself. Rather, articulated within its incompleteness is an ethical obligation, a right and a responsibility, to question the fruits of research and its intellectual and physical labour. Education demands horizons of open accountability to an other unforeseeable limit whose boundaries are never ending, never in sight. It has to engage in an ethical questioning that aims to rethink the interests of science and the course of *paideia* arising out of the transitions from past to present knowledges that exist as disciplinary formations. A call to a heightened sense of academic responsibility within the practices of scientific inquiry, their teaching and learning looks toward a future of research as a curriculum *yet-to-come*, as examples of a sustained critique that settles around the problem of *what it means to know* in relation to the epistemological field of technology, the crisis of legitimation after modernism, and the rule of language. The traditional notion of academic responsibility that is tied to the pursuit of truth via a conception of science is based on the teleological orientation of intellectual labour. An aim toward the production of tangible outcomes achieved according to a method of procedural objectivity.

For Jacques Derrida, this is not an insignificant developmental history because its effects determine the nature of the epistemic subjectivity of the researcher. And the nature of academic responsibility in the name of scientific progress and therefore the progress of human learning. The ethics and politics of research – and the role of the educational institution in helping to construct the dimensions of a scholastic arena for a *paideia* constructed on the premise of human progress through scientific inquiry – has called for the pragmatic application of research results, or the 'pay off' of pre-directed outcomes of inquiry solidified in curriculum. A result that is fed more and more by competing interests situated outside of the rationale of the institution itself. Most certainly, academic work programmed and organized solely on the future expectation of its profitable use, does not and cannot take into account the democratic ideal of protecting the welfare of the nation-state and the rights of its citizens. Especially when the quest for knowledge becomes driven by particularized and exclusionary agendas that arbitrarily guide the course of inquiry for political or economic reasons. A myopic orientation to research as an instrumental process of usable outcomes for human progress limits intellectual freedom and responsibility because it is, Derrida has contended, 'centered instead on [the desires of] multinational military-industrial complexes of techno-economic networks, or rather international technomilitary networks that are apparently multi- or trans-national in form'.[2] Indeed, such regulatory forces wielding the power of 'in-vest-ment' – not necessarily monetary – are always wanting to control the mechanisms of creative production and education. Knowledge is commodified so as to make it a useful product of pre-ordained and pre-conceived epistemological directives and scientific outcomes not necessarily for the sake of science, truth or knowledge. These 'external' influences affecting and reflecting the purposes of education are to be found more and more in not so obvious, but covertly strategic, areas within the architectonic confines of the traditional institutional structure. This is possible thanks to the channelling of interests that have penetrated the epistemological sphere and are therefore indispensable to the logic of its goals and operation. In fact, the direction and scope of research within and throughout the university are guided by the irresistible lure of funding and other personal and professional incentives arising therefrom (e.g. power, status, career advancement, etc.). And yet, to intimate, as I have, that the 'pragmatic' (utilitarian) interests of an 'applied science' are in opposition to the relative disinterestedness of 'fundamental' (basic) inquiry is to create a binary distinction. A qualitative and evaluative division of research along these lines is, without a doubt, problematic. The ethics of its logic is something that deconstruction has shown, can and should consistently be worked against. Derrida reminds us, however, that such a metaphysical conceit separating theory and practice is of 'real but limited relevance'.[3] Given that the deferred dividends of the 'detours, delays and relays of "orientation", its more random aspects',[4] are either incalculable or go unrecognized until a suitable situation of the advantageous use of research presents itself. The use-value of research cannot be an unimportant consideration. The ethics of science and its endeavours quickly occupies the foreground of analysis as the purpose of knowledge discovery comes into question. For Derrida, it is naïve to believe there are some 'basic disciplines ["philosophy", "theoretical physics", and "pure mathematics" are the examples he gives] shielded from power, inaccessible to programming by the pressures of the State or, under cover of the State, by civil society or capital interests'.[5] That thought has now been unthinkable for some time. It has been made obvious by the monstrous dawning of the 'post-critical' age of nuclear politics and its aftermath: the function of science as research '[a]t the service of war'.[6] In this sense, what has been at stake with respect to the purpose of research in all of its manifestations is the mode of conquering the symbiotic field of human and non-human concerns. That is, the race to 'control' knowledge and the industry resulting from the commodification of its results as intellectual by-products to be used by the State apparatus. This desire to command the path and ethics of science has and will pivot around the 'higher priority' issue of protecting 'national and international security'[7] interests for the progress of the State, however heterogeneous the calculation of a plan of research (or the lack of it) is to the logic of 'peace' or 'democracy'.

The differentiation of the aims of research is not that discreet an indicator of its 'use-value' so as to clearly distinguish between the profitability of application and the destructive effects of misappropriation, despite the usual factoring-in of 'reasonable' margins of error. Derrida comments,

> [...] research programs have to [in the sense of, *are made to*] encompass the entire field of information, the stockpiling of knowledge, the workings and thus also the essence of language and of all semiotic systems, translation, coding and decoding, the play of presence and absence, hermeneutics, semantics, structural and generative linguistics, pragmatics, rhetoric. I am accumulating all these disciplines in a haphazard way, on purpose, but I shall end with literature, poetry, the arts, fiction in general: the theory that has all these disciplines as its object may be just as useful in ideological warfare as it is in experimentation with variables in all-too-familiar perversions of the referential function. Such a theory may always be put to work in communications strategy, the theory of commands, the most refined military pragmatics of jussive utterances (by what token, for example, will it be clear that an utterance is to be taken as a command in the new technology of telecommunications? How are the new resources of simulation and simulacrum to be controlled? And so on [...]) [...] Furthermore, when certain random consequences of research are taken into account, it is always possible to have in view some eventual benefit that may ensue from an apparently useless research project (in philosophy or the humanities, for example). The history of the sciences encourages researchers to integrate that margin of randomness into their centralized calculation. They then proceed to adjust the means at their disposal, the available financial support, and the distribution of credits. A State power or forces that it represents no longer need to prohibit research or to censor discourse, especially in the West. It is enough that they can limit the means, can regulate support for production, transmission, diffusion.[8]

Within the 'concept of information or informatization',[9] the ethics and the politics of research take shape, essentially as the conservative ideal of 'Science' the university itself stands on is overtaken by external interests. The transformation of research goals and purposes consumes the institution because the autonomy of its own self-regulating measures of knowledge advancement is sacrificed to the real-world pressures of simply securing a sustainable future for itself as an economically and politically viable institution of culture. And that is understandable. Although it may not be ethically defensible or acceptable. Not even to those unquestioning defenders of the dominant interpretation of the principle of reason and science the university is grounded on to serve market interests. Essentially, by its logic of 'integrat[ing] the basic to the oriented, the purely rational to the technical, thus bearing witness to that original intermingling of the metaphysical and the technical'[10] within the disciplinary corpus of the institution.

Any pedagogical undertaking – and by extension any teaching body – is rendered accountable by law to what is taught and how as the disciplinary expression of cultural content and form within a curriculum of learning. Yet to understand what is at stake for the future of education as an effect of the cultural auditing of *knowledge-in-formation*, we must ask an impossible question: Does knowledge have to be reduced to a curricular archive in order to make education the product and practice of a teachable certainty as the truth of culture and the reality of its representations? The most obvious answer is: 'yes'. But is it possible not to limit the truth of knowledge to a single and finite trajectory of meaning within the idea of a curriculum? Only if we bring the concept of curriculum to a closure – not an end – and begin to audit the inflections of our epistemological investment in the notion of curriculum so as to rethink the goals and objectives of education, although without a silly yearning for a future that would deny *what-is-to-come* after the idea of curriculum.

The suggestion will seem ludicrous for some and welcome to others, which is not surprising considering all that has been secured in the concept of curriculum as *knowledge-in-formation*. It is a way to legitimize and guide the path and structure of disciplinarity in a mode of transmission while making sense of the educational project as an enterprise of auditing, representing and celebrating the re-learning of a culture. A curriculum – constituted by an evidentiary document and its mode of praxis – inheres both knowledge and non-knowledge in what it includes and excludes. The distinctions are arbitrary but temper the boundaries of free choice by filtering subjective judgements through an archive of recognized disciplinary achievement and authorized research designed to guide *knowledge-in-formation*. There are principles of valuation that actively govern the instauration of knowledge and its institution within a scene of teaching. The educational landscape of the West is played out against the backdrop of a conceptual legacy that has invested the pedagogical imperative with an ideological subtext promoting an ethic of infinite progress bound up in a quest for personal discovery and self-betterment called lifelong learning. The journey toward the intellectual perfectibility of the self is thought to be driven by a dauntless epistemological curiosity. After Kant, Jacques Derrida has identified the idealist presupposition of an impetus in educational theory that has 'aim[ed] at the total, perfect political unification of the human species *(die vollkommene bürgerliche Vereinigung in der Menschengattung)*'.[11] Institutions like UNESCO support the premise by attempting to secure the right to education for all through a single governing body. Derrida's notion of the cosmopolitical undoes the Eurocentric bias of universalism within globalization and the UNESCO experiment, *not only* as a way to reconceptualize *being-in-the-world*, but as a new approach to realizing the impossible futures of a 'progressive institutionality' to come and the unforeseeability of its educational methods and apparatus. This does not simply mean a securing of the opportunity for freedom in thinking and teaching; neither does it defer pedagogically, nor ethically, to the teaching of thinking without reference to the tradition of Western episteme, however it may be defined in curricular terms. The notion of the cosmopolitical subject, the resulting consequence of a new global hybridity, reawakens and resituates the Eurocentrism of the concept of the autonomous subject and its implications for reinscribing the 'horizon of a new community' of the question and the impossibility of the question that teaches the Other to question the sources of the Self and the Other. This may sound strange to those who envision and portray deconstruction as a *destruction* of Western metaphysics, its institutions and its teachings. We need to remember, however, the case of UNESCO as an institution that is *a priori* Kantian in spirit. Which is to say, it *predicts* a Western trajectory of thinking along a teleological axis with respect to the epistemologico-cultural ideal of the 'infinite progress' of Being and the temporal procession of beings toward perfectibility, achievable or not. Anything else would be a fantasy given the inseparability of the European history of philosophy from the notion of the universal. In the process, educational institutions become accountable for the future of a society and the survival of the State because of the power of curriculum to influence the minds, hearts and bodies of a new generation.

As an archive of privileged *knowledge-in-formation*, a curriculum presupposes the possibility of reducing teaching and learning to a set of mental decoding operations and performative outcomes that are empirical and therefore measurable of the cognitive and habitual changes within consciousness. This is the scientific definition of education. Knowledge is nothing if it is not grounded upon the possibility of a permanent record of physical data that can then be verified according to the 'laws of science' articulated as the demonstrable evidence of the self-certainty of the truth and method of research. The proof of learning is in the practice of transmitting and reproducing an archive of information always already sanctioned by the historicity of cultural institutions. This evaluative criterion constituting the comprehensible input and output of knowledge puts limits on teaching and learning that allows for the discipline of a curriculum to be neatly enjoined to pedagogical method, thus producing the possibility of *knowledge-in-formation* as a directed practice. Education depends upon the feasibility of referring to relatively stable archives of meaning to endow expressions of understanding with the evidence of empirical value and predictive power when it comes to constructing the elements of cognition. The failings of conscious memory in teaching and learning over time require the continuing, verifiable proof of a past and a future to secure the possibility of a genealogical rendering of human experience through pedagogy.

So, to mourn the death of curriculum resonates as premature. The nostalgia to recapture a moment of perfect and perfectible memory outside of time and space mistakenly presupposes a common and universal recognition of the end of an epistemic tradition rooted in the rise of the Occident as an archive of teaching and learning. The *force* of this mourning of curriculum mobilizes and is mobilized by a lamentation of the violence perpetrated against the Archaeology of the Letter, its *arkhe and telos*, the beginning and the finale of the history of metaphysics. Regret for the 'pure loss',[12] Derrida reminds us, of an *ideal consignment of knowledge* leaves a space (*kenosis*) for the possibility of an assembling or *gathering (Versammlung), a coming together*, of that which would mark the scene of a new beginning onto the futures of thinking, teaching and learning, with no programmable end in sight. But still in relation to a cultural archive of knowledge constructing the curricular basis for disciplinarity. Nostalgia forecloses creative invention by throwing back subjectivity into memory and an idealized imagining of the past. What will therefore arise *from within* the irreducible anteriority of the somatico-psychic experience of 'curriculum' from a backward looking perspective is an ineffable opening of metaphysics itself, unto the threshold of an impossible unfolding of lost time.[13] There is no sense in dealing with an unforeseeable future for education from a nostalgia to forget the past. This causes curriculum to be re-founded '*à corps perdu*',[14] passionately, impetuously, with desperation, Derrida would say. So as to attempt to master the outside limits of knowledge and the inexhaustive multiplicity of its sub-versive domain comprising the instantiation of philosophy in action on both sides of a well-defined margin we call curricular:

> Which does not amount to acknowledging that the margin maintains itself within *and* without. Philosophy says so too: *within* because philosophical discourse [inhered within the discourse of curriculum] intends to know and to master its margin, to define the line, align the page, enveloping it in its volume. *Without* because the margin, *its* margin, *its* outside are empty, are outside: a negative without effect in the text *or* a negative working in the service of meaning, the margin *relevé* (*aufgehoben*) in the dialectics of the Book. Thus one will have said nothing, or in any event done nothing, in declaring 'against' philosophy [as curriculum] that its margin is within or without, within and without, simultaneously the inequality of its internal spacings and the regularity of its borders.[15]

A hyper-idealized vision that beckons the end of curriculum, not its deconstruction, looks forward to an epistemological breakthrough of infinite possibility. It calls for the restoration of a new order beyond the encyclopaedia of tradition that sustains the illusion of having any connections to 'a past' by leaving behind or ignoring the historicity of a body of thought and thinking. Such a reaction can only be 'natural' (read uncritical). The *phthora*, a fraying, untangling or wearing-away in degradation, of the spatio-temporal organization of the structurality of the archive, after all, destabilizes the dimensions of the decisive and indivisible set of points tracing the hieratic lineage of the *meaning of metaphysics, the metaphysics of meaning*. In the process, it minimizes the already myopic perspective and perspicacity of those hoping to actualize those first steps of faith toward the enactment of an impossible time – a post-curricular era.[16]

A word of caution, however, is worth mentioning here as it distinguishes the two horns of the dilemma: the *ouverture* of metaphysics and the fathomability of its Other. To conjugate the problem of curriculum, once again, both as the pathology of the *mal d'archive* and as the madness of the repetition compulsion, though in a different manner, we become concerned more with the future of curriculum and less fixated on the altogether moribund mourning for the death of curriculum. On the one hand, all expenditures made to secure a future (for) thinking after the recognition of the impermanence, or *the lack*, of an absolute archive of thought must rely on the aim to 'coordinate a single corpus, in a system or a synchrony'[17] of repeatable structures. And hence, to settle the foundation of a soci-ety, its com-mun-ity, its laws and institutions, what it values and teaches, protects: in short, to *make real* the desire to consummate, once again, the hospitality of THE DOMICILE (*oikia*), where 'we' could live and *be-at-home-in-being.* On the other, the reconstruction of the ground of the public sphere – the cosmopolitical[18] – is compelled to take place with and against the recesses of memory (*mneme, anamnesis, hypomnema*) after the work of mourning is done, though not yet finished, and provides solace in relief of what Derrida calls the *an-archontic*, an-archival, tendency. The movement toward a dismantling of the system of hierarchical order leaves us open to *the impression of a 'cleanbreak', a breach or rupture, of the history of the archive, of philosophy and its teaching.*[19] The contradiction of attempting to 'close-off' or put metaphysics 'between brackets' (*entre crochets*),[20] to try to exclude it while still having to retain *ipso facto* the mnemonic trace of its operating principles within the ground of curriculum in order to move beyond metaphysics, to OVERCOME it,[21] soon becomes evident. And so there is a false consciousness of the loss of the archive – the death of curriculum. The self-deluding internalization of a condition of separation, as a self-limiting idea supporting the turmoil that feeds the fever of a mourning for the death of curriculum, is destructive: essentially because the focus is put on *the end* rather than *the closure* of curriculum.[22] There is no sense of respect for the alterity of what *may* or *could* come after the prolonged completion of the idea of curriculum and its metaphysics of terminal ideas and action. Repetition creates difference and something other than the ends of curriculum. Rather, its deferral is inaugurated as the pedagogical practice of philosophy in action through the extended path of the ontological quest to counter the forgetting of Being by guiding the subject back to its true and noble nature through education.

Curriculum is designed to bring about the pedagogical unconcealment of *aletheia*, or truth, and to secure its unforgetting, by attempting to recall back into cultural and epistemic memory the conceptualization of the Spirit of being and its perfected essence as a science of the knowledge of being, defined after early Greek thinking as the self-presence of presence totally present to itself.[23] For this well-rounded circularity was the beginning and the end of philosophy in action as curriculum. Tensions between the 'unknowable weight'[24] of competing desires set to fill the chaos of the apocalyptic impression of a lack of a secure ground, and hence the absence of meaning for the subject, lead to the seductive awakening of a reconstructive drive singularly bent toward facilitating a 'return to order' and therefore to nature as an escape from a state of *athesis, non-positionality*, limbo.[25] All of these words most certainly are synonyms for death, the non-being of Being, and the *agon* of its metaphysical *aporia*.[26] A denegation of the genealogy of 'the Idea' and its ideo-logy does not recognize, however, that the legacy of curriculum can never be fully erased from cultural memory. The imprimatur of its diachronic sign traces the borderlines of Western thought on both sides of the limit between what divides knowledge and its other. The struggle to reinstitute curriculum is a fight against the renunciation of that which we desire to *keep close to home* because it is familiar (*heimliche*), familiarity itself – where 'we' live and dwell pedagogically as a teaching body. The desire is saturated with the sense of the need to identify a metalanguage for educational practices, and to sustain its dominant influence by externalizing the devastating effects of losing a stable centre of meaning, whereby an excessive melancholia results from the (post)modern subject losing faith in its semiotico-psychic attachments to an ordered conception of life-world (*Lebenswelt*) 'bit by bit' (*Einzeldurchführung*).[27]

And yet would or should we ever call for, or celebrate the death of curriculum – if such a thing could indeed be 'celebrated', welcomed in its popularization? Since the enclosure of curriculum and its metaphysics in a frame of perfect finitude places restrictions on the possibility and impossibility of engaging thinking at the outer limits of truth. And for good reason. Taking the *step (not) beyond (pas au-delà)* curriculum cannot likely be accomplished (from) without of curriculum, if it can be accomplished at all (which is really another way of saying it cannot!). This is the *aporia of passage* that must be negotiated with the aid of deconstruction and its risky strategy of an *ex-orbit-ant* modality of reading. A deconstructive strategy marks the double bind of the logic of each and any attempt to *transgress* or even, in some instances, *arrest the progress of the idea of curriculum and its metaphysics, whatever this may mean to a future of thinking about education that has always already been in a perpetual state of closure and therefore without end.* The route to new forms of knowledge is characterized by this *ethical* and paradoxical problem of the lack of an outside: *paradox*, from its rootedness in the Greek, *paradoxon*, meaning a thinking beyond popular opinion (*doxa*) yet placed within the hyper-teleology of duty, the right (*orthotes*), of what can or cannot be *justly glorified*, deserves to be held up as an exemplary model to be emulated because it is at once a singular exception, a rare or impossible occurrence, worthy of praise, *doxastic*. The law of this antinomy represented by the image of the '*hors-texte*', whose double reading Derrida has used to identify the illusion of exteriority, the *Il n'y a pas* of an 'out-text'/the non-presence of an '*outside-of-the-text*', thus structures the inconsolability of the desire to *withdraw from* curriculum so as to regain the essence of subject-ivity and re-claim the spirit of Being in the name of difference and its radicalization of heterogeneity: e.g. the multitudinal guises of a negative and relational locality actualized by the term 'Otherness'.[28] And this may seem a strange and perhaps scandalous indictment, especially to those who have struggled in good faith, yet blindly, to overturn universalism for the purpose of instating particularity. Only to find that via the cultural/material space of an inscription of identity for its own sake, essentialism quickly dissipates the ethical necessity of recognizing and responding to the alterity of an Other with/in the Selfsame. The struggle to escape curriculum, however precautionary its measures and forthrightness of purpose (good faith, ethicity, openness), will always fail outright because its closure is by definition interminable, a process of repeated repetitions, alterity, a variegation without ending or end. The incommensurability between this lack of an opening and the overzealous push to enforce a moment of finality becomes the enigmatic centre of the paradox that suspends curriculum amid mirrored images of its past achievements and the impossible dreams of its future glory as the end of education. But then, the ethical questioning of the trajectory of curriculum and its hyper-genealogical aftermath beyond end and closure still persists. It proceeds: mainly, along the *peras* or axis of these guiding lines. Questions persist. Is the fate of curriculum doomed to pursue in vain the eschatological struggle of attempting to efface the traces of itself so as to break free from the onto-ideologico-epistemic archive of past and present knowledges? To effectively look forward to bringing about its own death in order to recreate itself anew by seeking to step beyond and by doing so step/not beyond the ground of metaphysics and its institutions? Is knowledge without curriculum possible? Desirable? Can there be a closure or/and an end of curriculum? And would this constitute an ethical crisis for curriculum and its archaeo-logical institution that is disseminated and regulated culturally as/in a form of teaching and learning? And what of its pedagogy? *The right of its pedagogy both as form and content.* Who would have the *right to teaching and learning*, the *right to education* and its 'other heading', *the right of its other heading*? These are no doubt difficult questions. Impossible interrogations, *aporias* we could assuredly call them with some confidence of the designation. In relating as they do to the history of education and its institution via the concept of curriculum. I must consequently disarm myself of any claims to knowledge presumptuous of 'final solutions' and its liberal affectations of a teleological exodus of sorts. The force of the questioning cannot subside, however, and be absorbed in the paralyzing desire for an end-thought, an end to/of thought. Because it simply will not happen that I will solve the riddle of *finding a way out of curriculum*. It would be wiser, and surely ethical enough, to forgo any such analytico-idealistic aspirations from the start, so as to prepare the path for the possibility of an affirmation arising from *within* or *through* the *aporia* of a non-passage, to what may lie beyond the borders of curriculum yet remains ensconced in its haunt.[29] This disarmament, curiously enough, therefore, also constitutes a necessary precaution, much needed *guardrails* to work against and, if possible, to exceed, Derrida would say, and thereby re-marking the dangerous boundaries of the 'limits of truth' where the solid ground of reason gives way to the undecidability of the abyss, an *ur-ground* perhaps of an-other type, an impossible one, itself being grounded, like deconstruction, in an un-grounding of its groundedness (e.g. presence as absence or lack, neither emptiness nor a void). If I were wholly bound by a finite sense of the debt owed to the scholarly duty of attempting *at all costs* to reach terminal – rather than provisional – conclusions that are intended to 'wrap up' research and halt discussion, I would not be predisposed to what may unexpectedly announce itself out of my re-reading of the concept of curriculum and the ethics of its body of teaching, also of its teaching body (*corps enseignant*). Still, it is not a matter of throwing all caution to the wind in order to make laudable pronouncements.

With Derrida and the deconstruction of logocentrism, we are cognizant of the need to move to new ground now, after and out of the path of idealism and ontology, to proceed ethically with and beyond the debt and duty owed to the archaeo-logical excavations of a past time. Only through a responsible questioning that rises out of what is said and left unsaid in the Western tradition of metaphysics can a reaffirmation of 'curriculum' as the interpretational moment of a disciplinary line of inquiry, as the translation of an institutional framework, and as the enactment of a pedagogy potentially occur. Derrida – and I will have reiterated the following before – has consistently tried to make an epistemic shift in thinking about education away from questions of ontology and truth that are predicated on a classical thinking of difference, to problems of de-ontology and the affirmative ethics of *différance*. Deconstruction weighs in heavily here as a remarkable theory of education, teaching and learning, a novel way to rethink curriculum, and as 'an institutional practice for whom the concept of institution remains a problem'.[30] Essentially, the problem of curriculum is the case of envisioning the completion of the subject, *what it is* and *what it could be*, in its self and in its relation with others. Traditionally, this has meant not only conceptualizing an intellectual and corporeal end to teaching but an endpoint to education as a formal course of pedagogical action and its academic responsibility to questions of truth and knowledge. The difficulty with projecting the completion of the subject is that curriculum forecloses the identity of the empirical subject and replaces it with an ideal one, a *what* instead of a *who*. Educational structures depersonalize curriculum for the sake of the efficient delivery of knowledge in the name of common results articulated as objectives, goals and aims. The collective mediation of a student body thus supersedes the process of subjective self-actualization that pedagogy seeks to engender, thus resulting in a fixation of the teaching body on method for its own sake. Any curriculum cannot but fail to effectuate any disclosure of the self that is uniquely personal enactment. Curriculum guides teaching by posing the question '*What* is the subject I want to develop?' If the subject is produced through directed action, the subject is singular, not collective. Not a 'what', but a 'who'. The subject is particular in its relation to the other and the ground of intersubjectivity is determined via *praxis*. Subjectivity discloses itself in accordance with its determination by an other who engages the self within the communicative sphere of discourse and action toward the imperative of understanding the absent ground of otherness that radicalizes difference. Curriculum is the methodological value of experience translated as pedagogical guidance. Its application toward the formation of an ideal subjectivity reiterates the nostalgia of the desire to confirm the empirical and theoretical grounds of knowledge that allows us to understand each other as subjects in a culture when we engage the difference of other subjectivities. Curriculum foreshadows reciprocity. But it posits a closed system of exchanges that go back and forth in a circular fashion of a perfect communication. In actuality, we learn more about ourselves when we engage the other; we learn more about the other when we engage ourselves. A radicalization of curriculum ensues: if subjectivity is discovered in action and intersubjectivity is born in the coming to presence of the subject through the engagement of an other, then the contextual application of a generalizable curriculum to facilitate the actualization of subjectivity is misguided and unethical. The practice of education works itself out in relation to the larger context of a community of difference that is always already absent, yet to be realized, and on the horizons of an impossible trajectory for where the knowledge of the Self and selfhood encounters multiple sites of understanding.

The ethical moment of this opening of location and locality, the space and place, *khorismos* and *khora*, is what Derrida calls the cosmopolitical debt and duty to reconsider the ground of our knowledge. Engaging the cosmopolitical means facilitating a return to questions of academic responsibility in hopes of transforming the ground of thinking and practice with the past always in mind. This is vital in its importance for what is at stake – that is, for the future of education and curriculum itself. Despite its wanting 'to reach the point of a certain exteriority [non-closure, alterity or otherness] in relation to the totality of the age of logocentrism'[31] that habituates education as curriculum, deconstruction nevertheless must remain hopelessly and forever tied to the normative discourse of curriculum, loyal to the epistemic history of the knowledge that it questions. It perseveres at taking an affirmative line of questioning with respect to the reductive formulizability of binary thought that fixes the subject and establishes a hyper-simplistic, teleo-idiomatic construction of the ontological difference of identity in both conceptual and empirical terms. Deconstruction, whether it wants to or not, redefines the conditional determinacy of the axiological limits to thinking that it meets and will ultimately test. It converges upon uncharted destinations of thinking, teaching and learning without the confines of a ready-made (*etymon*), contextualized map. It has a nostalgia for the past that is used to build a knowledge of the other upon without an ideal memory. Deconstruction challenges the curricular ground of an inalterable archive that specifies 'what knowledge is of most worth'. Its duty to question what is held sacred, taken for granted as **TRUTH** (always in boldly capital letters), even venerated, risks both *all* and *nothing* because of its open responsibility to the Other whose effects on the formation of the subject and subjectivity are incalculable. Deconstruction reduces the proximity of the subject to the difference of the other by opening up the venues of epistemic memory and pedagogical action that blaze trails to new knowledges and institutions which can enable the invention of new forms of seeing, listening and hearing the other within the differences that bind us in mind and body to a nostalgia of envisioning a future after the idea of curriculum.

Notes

[1] Jean Baudrillard, 'The Violence of the Global', trans. François Debrix, *Ctheory* (March, 2003).

[2] Jacques Derrida, 'The Principle of Reason: The University in the Eyes of its Pupils', *Diacritics* (Fall, 1983), p.11. 'The Principle of Reason', we must remember, was written and presented in April of 1983. At the time – the peaking of the 'Cold War' – this is a fair description of the homogeneous 'conditionality' of the Western 'nation-states' – most conspicuously exemplified by America and Russia – that according to Derrida were spending in total upwards of 'two million dollars a minute' on the manufacture of armaments alone.

[3] Derrida, 'The Principle of Reason', p.12.

[4] Derrida, 'The Principle of Reason', p.12.

[5] Derrida, 'The Principle of Reason', p.12.

[6] Derrida, 'The Principle of Reason', p.13.

[7] Derrida, 'The Principle of Reason', p.13.

[8] Derrida, 'The Principle of Reason', p.13.

[9] Derrida, 'The Principle of Reason', p.14.

[10] Derrida, 'The Principle of Reason', p.14.

[11] Cited in Jacques Derrida, 'The Right to Philosophy from the Cosmopolitical Point of View (the Example of an International Institution)', in Jacques Derrida and Peter Pericles Trifonas [ed], *Ethics, Institutions, and the Right to Philosophy*, trans. Peter Pericles Trifonas (Lanham, MD: Rowan and Littlefield, 2002), p.6.

[12] See Jacques Derrida, *Archive Fever: A Freudian Impression*, trans. Eric Prenowitz (Chicago: University of Chicago Press, 1996).

[13] See Jacques Derrida, *Aporias*, trans. Thomas Dutoit (Stanford: Stanford University Press, 1993); Jacques Derrida, *The Gift of Death*, trans. David Wills (Chicago: University of Chicago Press, 1995).

[14] Jacques Derrida, 'Tympan', in *Margins of Philosophy*, trans. Alan Bass (Chicago: University of Chicago Press, 1982), p.xxiii.

[15] Derrida, 'Tympan', p.xxiv.

[16] See Derrida, *Aporias*.

[17] Derrida, *Archive Fever*, p.3.

[18] See Jacques Derrida, *Le droit à la philosophie du point de vue cosmopolitique* (Paris: Éditions UNESCO, Verdier, 1997). All translated passages are citations from this text.

[19] See Derrida, *Archive Fever*.

[20] Jacques Derrida, 'Between Brackets I', in Elizabeth Weber [ed], *POINTS ... Interviews, 1974–1994*, trans. Peggy Kamuf (Stanford: Stanford University Press, 1995), pp.5–29.

[21] See Martin Heidegger, 'The End of Philosophy and the Task of Thinking', trans. David Farrell Krell, in David Farrell Krell [ed] *Martin Heidegger: Basic Writings* (San Francisco: HarperCollins Publishers, 1977), pp.373–392.

[22] On the relationship between death, memory, mourning and the archive of metaphysics as the cinders of fire and fever marking an opening to the trace of the Other, see Derrida, *Archive Fever*, and Jacques Derrida, *Cinders*, trans. Ned Lukacher (Lincoln & London: University of Nebraska Press, 1987).

[23] See Heidegger, 'The End of Philosophy'.

[24] Derrida, *Archive Fever*, p.29.

[25] See Derrida, *Cinders*; Jacques Derrida, *The Post Card: From Socrates to Freud and Beyond*, trans. Alan Bass (Chicago: University of Chicago Press, 1987); and most recently Jacques Derrida, *Resistances of Psychoanalysis*, trans. Peggy Kamuf, Pascale-Anne Brault and Michael Naas (Stanford: Stanford University Press, 1998) for a discussion of the relationship between the death drive and the pleasure principle and how deconstruction interacts with psychoanalysis.

[26] See Jacques Derrida, *Of Spirit: Heidegger and the Question*, trans. Geoffrey Bennington and Rachel Bowlby (Chicago: University of Chicago Press, 1989).

[27] See Derrida, *Aporias* and *The Post Card*.

[28] An interesting discussion of this aspect of deconstruction can be found in (among other places) Derrida, *Aporias*; Jacques Derrida, 'Violence and Metaphysics', in *Writing and Difference*, trans. Alan Bass (Chicago: University of Chicago Press, 1978),

pp.79–153; and the farewell and final tribute Derrida expressed to Emmanuel Levinas. An English version of that testimonial and oration was published as Jacques Derrida, 'Adieu', *Philosophy Today* 40:3 (1996), pp.330–340.

[29] Refer to Derrida, *Aporias.*

[30] Derrida, *Du droit à la philosophie* (Paris: Galilée, 1990), p.88. (All translations from this text are my own.)

[31] Jacques Derrida, *Of Grammatology*, trans. Gayatri Chakravorty Spivak (Baltimore: Johns Hopkins University Press, 1974), pp.161–162.

Peter Pericles Trifonas is a professor at the Ontario Institute for Studies in Education at the University of Toronto. Some of his most recent books are *Ethics, Institutions, and the Right to Philosophy* with Jacques Derrida, *Barthes and the Empire of Signs*, and *Communities of Difference.*

parallax, 2004, vol. 10, no. 2, 50–62

High Performance Schooling

Jon McKenzie

*A faculty member at Columbia University spoke of a friend who
was planning to begin graduate studies after having been out of
school several years. The professor asked whether she was anxious
about the Graduate Record Examination, a standardized test
required for admission to graduate school. 'Well,' was the response,
'I'm an American. I was born to be tested.'*
F. Allan Hanson, *Testing Testing*[1]

As anthropologist Marilyn Strathern notes in her introduction to the collection *Audit Cultures*, the emergence of audit and assessment procedures that we see in academic practice 'is part of a global phenomenon. Audit regimes accompany a specific epoch in Western international affairs'.[2] The different evaluative procedures found in the US GRE (Graduate Record Examination) and the UK RAE (Research Assessment Exercise) are both culturally specific – and increasingly shared by people around the world. From individuals and small groups to larger institutions, governments and, of late, international and transnational organizations, we find a complex and growing regime of evaluative procedures that accompany, enable and, precisely, *account* for contemporary processes of globalization. Such procedures are in no way limited to academics, of course, but extend across every social sphere, including those of business, politics, healthcare, the military and even art and culture. Through initiatives such as the United Nation's Global Compact, the entire world is becoming a giant test site, a colossal 'audit-orium' or space of auditing. Perhaps a more fitting punch line to my epigraph will soon be: 'I'm an Earthling. I was born to be audited'.

It is tempting – and worthwhile – to understand the emergence of formal assessment procedures within the university as a recent and unprecedented intrusion of financial and managerial practices into the academy. Yet while it is important to distinguish, for instance, the academic examination and the financial audit, it may be equally important to analyze, assess, examine and, well, audit their commonalities. At the most general level, the exam and the audit are modern forms of evaluation, applicable to individuals and institutions alike. Similarly, while it is crucial to theorize the 'newness' of audit cultures around the globe (a task I shall attempt below), it is likewise important to recognize certain continuities with the past. As Max Weber suggested a century ago, the modern university is that bureaucracy which prepares people to work

parallax
ISSN 1353-4645 print/ISSN 1460-700X online © 2004 Taylor & Francis Ltd
http://www.tandf.co.uk/journals
DOI: 10.1080/1353464042000208512

in other bureaucracies. Accountants and auditors, for example, do not learn their trade solely in the workplace; they are first educated and trained in the academy, as are contemporary management consultants and 'performance gurus'. Weber himself stressed the importance of examinations for entrance into a wide variety of capitalist institutions; in addition, he noted that the 'bureaucratization of capitalism, with its demand for expertly trained technicians, clerks, et cetera, carries such examinations all over the world'.[3]

Global audit cultures, then, are both new and old, both highly 'financialized' and highly 'academicized'. Nonetheless, despite certain commonalities and continuities, the phenomenon of 'audit cultures' within contemporary educational institutions is both different from and discontinuous with previous forms of academic normalization. Contemporary audit and assessment procedures can be understood within the context of 'new managerialism', a much wider regime of organizational practices that must itself be seen as a crucial part of global neoliberal capitalism. And, as cited above, Strathern contends that audit regimes accompany a particular epoch in Western international affairs, adding that an 'anthropologist's question might be just how one recognizes epochal change'.[4]

My own purpose here is to offer a way of recognizing this epochal change, theorizing different dimensions of audit culture in terms of performance, or more specifically, in terms of a general theory of performance.[5] Performance provides not so much a unified perspective from which to theorize audit culture but instead a complex yet highly specific set of contrasting perspectives, among the most relevant here being 'financial performance', 'performance measurement', 'performance studies', 'performance management' and 'performativity'.

To begin with, one performance perspective that helps us to think through the question of audit culture is the increasingly global use of the term 'financial performance', used to analyze everything from stocks and bonds to corporations to entire markets and even global economies. Indeed, officials of the International Monetary Fund regularly assess 'global economic performance'.

From the perspective of critical cultural theory, financial performance functions as a highly normative paradigm of social discourse and provides us with critical tools for understanding the repressive regimes of audit cultures. But this is not the only use of the term performance that concerns us here. A very different perspective – some might say an *opposite* usage – comes from performance studies, a research paradigm that focuses on cultural performances ranging from theatre and ritual to performance art and expressive behaviours of everyday life. Performance studies scholars based in the US, UK, and increasingly around the world, tend to stress the resistant or transgressive potential of cultural performance and thus provide us with an oppositional perspective on audit culture. To think effectively about the cultural dimension of 'audit culture' might well be to use the terms put forward by the field of performance studies.

However salient both the normative performances of finance and the transgressive performances of culture may be for understanding audit cultures, I will argue that audit procedures found in the university are largely synonymous with contemporary 'performance measurement' techniques developed over the course of the 20th century in a wide range of organizations, from corporations to governments. There is widespread evidence that a major paradigm shift occurred within organizational theory and practice around the Second World War, producing what many practitioners and researchers now call 'performance management', a paradigm much more attuned to service and information work than the industrial labour studied by Taylor and thus more readily applicable to educational contexts. Simply put, performance management describes the new managerialism.

'Financial performance', 'performance studies' and 'performance management' are not simply different variations or meanings of the term 'performance'; rather, each entails specific sets of discourses and practices used by very different people – accountants and financial analysts, artists and cultural theorists, and managers and organizational theorists – working in very different contexts. Each has emerged in the United States since WWII and each has gone – or is currently going – global. Nonetheless, these different performance paradigms are now overlapping, intersecting and, more profoundly, constituting the epochal change suggested by Strathern. In this essay, I aim to give a general account of performativity and its relation to the academy. Though many of my examples come from the US, such an account has relevance to the British academy and many others, as well as to the broader topic of 'auditing culture', which I take to be a global, and indeed, globalizing phenomenon, one in which performativity plays a crucial and even leading role. Indeed, I contend that 'performance' is an emerging formation of power and knowledge, one that builds upon yet displaces the disciplinary formation described by Foucault. Or to put this another way: audit cultures arise in an age of global performativity.

Education and performativity

The relevance of performativity for understanding the emergence of audit cultures within the academy can be seen in Lyotard's *The Postmodern Condition: A Report on Knowledge*, first published in French in 1979 and translated into English in 1984. Let us recall Lyotard's central argument: modern philosophers and educators legitimated both knowledge and power through such 'grand narratives' as Enlightenment, Progress and Liberation. In contrast to modernity's grand, unified narratives, Lyotard argues that the postmodern entails diffuse language games. Specifically, he suggests that contemporary decision-makers 'attempt to manage these clouds of sociality according to input/output matrices, following a logic which implies that their matrices are commensurable and that the whole is determinable. They allocate our lives for the growth of power. In matters of social justice and of scientific truth alike, the legitimation of that power is based on its *optimizing the system's performance-efficiency*'.[6] Performativity, for Lyotard, is precisely system optimization, the incessant calculation or 'minimaxing' of input/output ratios (i.e. minimizing inputs and maximizing outputs), calculations greatly facilitated by computer and other information technologies. In some sense, performativity *is* the postmodern condition, and perhaps it follows that postmodern culture is an auditing culture.

While Lyotard's *Postmodern Condition* has long been one of the most influential articulations of postmodernism, his theorization of performativity's specific operation within the university was long overshadowed by the attention given to his more general considerations of the death of modernism's grand narratives. The global emergence of audit cultures, however, has brought renewed attention to Lyotard's discussion of education. Peter Roberts writes that an 'appraisal of the New Zealand policy scene suggests Lyotard was stunningly accurate in his predictions about many features of the changing higher education landscape'.[7] In particular, Roberts, writing in 1998, notes that 'there is much in the history of educational reform in New Zealand over the past 13 years that bears an uncanny resemblance to the scenario described so vividly by Lyotard nearly two decades ago. Several phases in the commodification of knowledge can be identified: the development of standardized units for trading qualifications (and parts of qualifications); the concentration on skills and information in curriculum policy; and, most importantly, the redefinition of the concept of "education" itself. Universities, along with all other tertiary institutions, are now expected to measure up to the new imperatives of performativity, and ongoing state support for programmes at odds with this logic cannot be guaranteed'.[8] That logic, again, is one of system optimization: optimizing both the operation of the educational system and, as importantly, its function within the broader economic system.

If Lyotard's theory of performativity appears prophetic with respect to the contemporary 'audit-oriums' of higher education, the ambiguities of performativity which Lyotard noted in passing have become more visible, numerous and troubling. Robin Usher and Nicky Solomon, two Australian education researchers, write that 'performativity contributes simultaneously to both the strengthening and loosening of boundaries, to both an economy of the same and to an economy of difference. This emphasis on performativity has contributed to a trend where researchers are held accountable for what they do through various forms of research assessment. Universities become more consumer oriented, dominated by a managerial discourse and a logic of accountability and excellence'.[9] Usher and Solomon argue that while the increased assessment of research may encourage the creation of elite researchers who work at elite universities, it may also be 'accompanied by a greater number of researchers and universities who previously didn't engage in scholarship and research in its traditional sense'.[10] Similarly, with respect to the types of research projects undertaken, they argue that performativity may in some instances restrict the range of research but in others increase the diversity of objects, methods and approaches.

Perhaps even more troubling than the diversity and ambiguity noted by Usher and Solomon is the possibility that even the most repressive versions of performativity actually *embrace* diversity, and that both the economies of sameness and those of difference increasingly serve the logic of capital. While Henry Ford once stated that people could buy a car in any colour they liked, '*as long as it is black*', today Toyota, BMW and General Motors not only manufacture cars in a wide array of colours, they also produce customized versions for more specialized tastes. And this embrace of difference is crucial, I would argue, to an understanding of audit cultures and global performativity.

Financial performance

Is it any coincidence that audit culture has emerged as a social phenomenon – or at least a critical concept – over the past decade or so, a decade that made the high rolling 80s look like a community centre BINGO game; a decade marked by the spread of new and highly popular, yet barely understood derivatives with such names as straddles, look back options and basket options; by what David Harvey has called the flexible accumulation of capital, the rapid and massive flows of financial investment into – and out of – far-flung international markets; by such troubling financial disasters as those surrounding Barings Bank, Long-Term Capital Management and the government of Orange County, California; by eye-popping returns on stocks, especially IPOs (initial public offerings) traded on an upstart market called NASDAQ; by speculative bubbles and spectacular busts in real estate, computers and telecommunications, the latter two not only providing exciting objects of speculation but also facilitating unprecedented means for doing so, such as online trading, day-trading and after-hours trading; and, finally, by scandals that rocked cutting-edge corporations, established investment banks and trusted accounting and auditing firms? From another perspective: to what extent could audit cultures *not* have emerged during such a financially driven time period?

We are witnessing the emergence of 'high performance finance', and its stakes are very high indeed. To take but one indication: the *Wall Street Journal*'s July 1, 2002 quarterly review section contained numerous charts ranking 'Best Performers' and 'Worst Performers'. The performers here were not high profile managers, much less famous actors or star athletes. In fact, the performers were not even human. Instead, the best and worst performers were financial instruments, market indexes and industrial sectors: the charts represented the second quarter performance of US-traded large-cap issues, US stock sectors, global stocks, global stock indexes and global industry groups.

The term 'performance' has become central to investors, stock brokers, financial analysts, government regulators and professional accountants and auditors. Whatever else stocks, bonds, mutual funds, markets, industries and economies do, today they all *perform*. For a term so central and ubiquitous to the financial world, it is striking that the definition of the term 'performance' remains elusive, not just for the casual investor or outside observer, but even and especially for financial professionals. This elusiveness became most evident during the 2002 scandals of leading corporations, investment companies and accounting and auditing firms. As early as February 26th of that year, the Financial Accounting Standards Board (FASB) convened a special task force on financial performance reporting by business enterprises. Its first discussion question: 'Is a definition of *financial performance* necessary or even desirable? More specifically, can financial performance be reduced to a single financial measure or a single financial statement?'

While the layperson might define financial performance simply as profitability or income, defining such profitability or income *accurately* and *consistently* is very problematic, as is representing financial performance in a formal statement. At issue are the criteria or measures that compose such performance. The FASB task force states that 'an assessment of a company's past performance and its prospects generally rely on benchmarks and comparisons to industry peers, which require, in part, external sources of information. Financial statements (and notes) certainly can provide measures of *operating* or *core* income, net income, comprehensive income, cash flows, total assets, revenue growth, debt to equity, return on equity and other financial measures that are useful in assessing performance. However, seeking to define financial performance might prove to be both unnecessary and a poor use of the Board's limited resources'.[11] While the task force acknowledges the possibility that a single statement might adequately report financial performance and implicitly suggests that 'net income' or 'operating income' is the critical criterion for determining financial performance, it explicitly refrains from defining the term.

The very difficulty of defining the concept 'performance' can, I believe, help us to see why it is important to investigate performance when we are theorizing audit culture. In its most technical sense, auditing is a fairly specific, recognizable task, one that is carried out by trained professionals. It is a term that can be used metaphorically, of course, and theorists of audit culture are interested in its roots, uses and displacements. But used in its financial sense, auditing is a term with a relatively clear definition. Performance, by contrast, multiplies and morphs, eludes definition in financial circles, and indeed, in other contexts. It appears in financial discourses, but it crops up across disciplines and fields of knowledge, meaning something different each time. And it appears on scales that are both larger and smaller than the audit. Auditors often measure 'performance', but then they are themselves measured as performers. Indeed, I would argue that performance is the term that swallows up both 'audit' and 'culture'. Unlike this pair of terms, yoked together as a new formulation, 'performance' is already widely deployed, being used to bring together both economics and culture. It allows us to think through the links between the normative evaluation of economic tasks and the production of a whole range of social activities and values precisely because the term 'performance' emerges in both economic and cultural environments, as if it belonged equally to both, and thus shows us how these worlds blur, overlap and connect. Thus although the concept of financial performance clearly connects us to the 'audit' of audit cultures, 'performance' describes an even more general regime of assessment and evaluation, one that absorbs 'audit' and 'culture' in ways that throws light on both.

Performance studies

This brings me to a second and very different sense of 'performance' that I wish to stress, one that comes out of the cultural sphere. The field of performance studies is a research paradigm that focuses on cultural performances, including theatre, ritual, performance art and practices of everyday life. Here performativity has traditionally meant a certain theatricality, expressivity or mimicry, though understood less as a form of entertainment and more as carrying some critical force or social efficacy, in particular that of opposition to dominant societal norms. This oppositional sense of performativity dates back to the 1960s, when artists, activists and scholars in the US and elsewhere sought to radicalize different forms of cultural performance within the context of the civil rights and anti-war movements. As Susan Stanford Friedman suggests, such radicalization continued in the following decades within the contexts of feminism, gay and lesbian activism, and post-colonial and critical race studies.[12]

This second, cultural, transgressive sense of performativity differs significantly from the financial performance discussed above, which is highly normative with respect to dominant societal standards. But it is worth noting here that performance studies shares at least two characteristics with financial performance. First, despite its emphasis on transgression, performance studies has itself become institutionalized as a recognizable discipline, complete with departments, publications, prizes and credentials; but, like financial performance, it is a discipline with boundaries which its scholars and practitioners find difficult to describe and delimit. Like its financial counterpart, the object of performance studies is itself elusive. Second, performance studies scholars, in prizing resistance and transgression, nonetheless *evaluate* cultural performances, often assessing them in terms of their social efficacy. They not only recognize the ways that cultural performances can transform social life; they assess how well and to what extent they do so. In short, like financial performance, performance studies is itself a plural field of objects to be evaluated, and, like Toyota or GM, embraces diversity while enforcing and enacting certain institutionalized norms.

Performance measurement and performance management

Let us shift to a third site where the term 'performance' is used, debated and contested. In 'The Performance Measurement Manifesto', management consultant and former Harvard Business School professor Robert G. Eccles writes that the 'leading indicators of business performance cannot be found in financial data alone. Quality, customer satisfaction, innovation, market share – metrics like these often reflect a company's economic condition and growth potential better than reported earnings do'.[13] In their 1984 *Performance Appraisal*, Evelyn Eichel and Henry E. Bender write that during 'the 1960s, the purpose of performance appraisal broadened to include development of the individual, organizational planning, and improving the quality of work life. Management now used performance appraisal to try to increase employee's productivity, effectiveness, efficiency, and satisfaction. Performance appraisal provided a basis for development of employee job skill, career planning, and motivation through effective coaching and information exchange between appraiser and appraisee'.[14]

Performance audits, performance reviews, performance appraisals, performance measurements – such evaluative procedures operate today within a large and powerful nexus of organizational discourses and practices called 'performance management'. Performance management can be best understood as a paradigm shift within organizational management, one that began in the mid-20th century in reaction to Frederick Taylor, who set out to rationalize manufacturing processes and improve individual workers' productivity through time and motion studies. Under scientific management, control of work shifted away from traditional foremen, who Taylor argued selected their workers based on loyalty rather than talent and who organized work according to informal rules of thumb rather than scientific methods. Over such foremen, Taylorism installed a new class of managers and specialists. Trained in the principles of scientific management, these mid-level managers and 'efficiency experts' sought to control factory workers with rationality, scientific method and strict conformity to the 'one best method'. Henry Ford's automobile factories stand as scientific management's emblematic achievement, and Taylor's *Principles of Scientific Management* helped to create a nation-wide 'efficiency craze' in the US. Taylor's techniques spread around the world, with even the Soviet Union making use of its principles.

By mid-century, however, a new management paradigm had begun to rival Taylorism, one that has become dominant today as highly developed economies have shifted from manufacturing to service and information industries. Rather than control workers, contemporary proponents of this new performance management paradigm stress the need to 'empower' them by developing their collaborative abilities, decision-making skills and creative talents for problem-solving and innovation. And performance management also addresses an extraordinarily wide definition of organization performance, from day-to-day operations, human resources and information technologies to strategic planning, executive leadership and decision-making, and underlying culture.

The rise of performance management not only entails changes in the function of performance measurement, but also in the scope of its application. Especially with the rise of such management schools as systems theory and information-processing and decision-making, performance measurement techniques began to be applied beyond individuals to work teams, departments and entire organizations. Information-processing and decision-making brought management fully into the performance measurement process, as managers themselves became subject to the very evaluative processes they once applied to labourers, while systems theory explicitly encompassed the entire organization, including non-human factors such as technologies and work environments. To give some sense of how expansive performance measurement has become: through the Clinton years, Vice-President Al Gore headed the National Performance Review, an annual assessment of US government departments and agencies. Significantly, such evaluative techniques were not only internalized by federal agencies. During the 1990s, the US Agency for International Development (USAID) developed formal 'Performance Monitoring Plans' to collect performance data on foreign countries applying for aid from the US government.

If performance management is widespread, difficult to pin down, and dedicated to the establishment of evaluative standards, one final aspect of this performance paradigm deserves special attention: its aesthetic or artistic dimension. In explicit contrast to scientific management, contemporary performance management often draws on models from the arts, valorizing intuition and creativity as much as rationality and analysis. The performing arts, and theatre in particular, have offered consultants and organizational theorists not only metaphors but fully developed conceptual models for theorizing alternative approaches to organizational management. Examples include Peter Vaill's *Managing as a Performing Art: New Ideas for a World of Chaotic Change*, Iain Mangham and Michael Overington's *Organizations as Theatre: A Social Psychology of Dramatic Appearances*, and Joseph Pine and James Gilmore's *The Experience Economy: Work Is Theatre & Every Business a Stage*.

Thus if performance management seems to echo the highly normative, economic imperatives of financial performance, it also incorporates the potentially emancipatory, exciting activity of cultural production. Like the first two, it unites both normativity and diversity, both evaluative procedures and the possibility of surprises. But more explicitly than either financial performance or performance studies, performance management seeks, quite deliberately, to fuse the activities of financial auditing and cultural performance. That is, it brings 'audit' and 'culture' into a single organizational model, and one that has significant global reach.

Global performativity

On the most general level, I would argue that performativity functions in the contemporary world much as Foucault argued that discipline functioned in the 18th and 19th centuries: as a specific onto-historical formation of power and knowledge, one that began to crystallize after the Second World War and is now becoming fully operational.[15] Whereas Foucault theorized the importance of disciplinary mechanisms for the production of the modern human subject and the functioning of such institutions as the hospital, prison and university, I contend that the emerging performance stratum entails, among other things, the displacement of human subjectivity and the blurring of institutional boundaries created under the reign of discipline. Indeed, to take examples from the paradigms of performance I have described above: financial models have intruded into the arts and the university, while paradigms of cultural performance have transformed management strategies. In every kind of contemporary 'performance' we may find evidence of such blurring: from orchestras to stock markets, from primary and secondary schools to healthcare, law enforcement and even the military.

While the disciplinary subject formation described by Foucault took place within relatively stable and self-contained institutional contexts, with subjects moving linearly from one to the next by crossing clearly demarcated thresholds (from school to army to factory to prison), performative subject formation occurs within mobile and overlapping evaluative grids. It can – and should – be noted that such institutional blurring is not really so new; Foucault's 'panopticonism', after all, refers to the displacement of Bentham's prison surveillance techniques to other institutions. What's unprecedented, however, is that today the displacement and blurring of institutional borders are themselves becoming codified if not 'institutionalized', and this development entails profound changes in processes of normalization. Disciplinary archives were comprised almost exclusively of analogue materials (records being primarily handwritten, typed, mimeographic or photographic) and were housed in discrete, stand-alone storage units such as file cabinets. By contrast, performative archives are increasingly digital and networked. Digitalization and networking allow virtually all media to be recorded and translated into the same binary code and the resulting records to be copied, transmitted, stored and accessed by different institutions. Further, data-mining and information-processing techniques give decision-makers potentially unlimited ways to research, cross-reference and analyze individuals' records or 'data bodies'. In part, due to this radical transformation in archiving, it is as if institutional borders are being breached from the inside out as well as from the outside in, with our data bodies now awaiting the arrival of our physical bodies. Specific institutions are still recognizable, of course, but both their archives and architectures bear traces of other institutions, and this hybridity produces subtle changes in one's expectations, behaviours and experiences. The Dartmouth-Hitchcock Medical Center down the road from me, for instance, has the look, feel and even the smell of an upscale shopping mall: carpeted, multi-storied arcades with skylights lead to shops and food courts as well as outpatient clinics and intensive care units. The medical centre serves patients from the college and the surrounding rural areas, and its different types of public spaces allow visitors from diverse social backgrounds to mix and interact. One visits the hospital and somewhere else at the same time. Similar architectural hybridity can be found in contemporary workplaces, museums, airports and schools. While the unified and centred subject produced by disciplinary normalization has not disappeared, the fractured, hyphenated and decentred individuals championed by many cultural theorists can no longer simply be valorized as inherently transgressive, critical and/or marginalized; rather, we must also begin to recognize them as potentially fully functioning, highly normalized performative subjects – as multi-tasking workers, eclectic consumers, multicultural citizens, interdisciplinary students, etc. – and even as all of these at once. If discipline operated through the integration of diversity, performativity entails the diversification of integration.

As politically influential and geographically extensive as all of these performance paradigms may be individually, *the performativity of contemporary globalization is best revealed by attempts to integrate different performative criteria*. We can see one attempt at integrating multi-paradigmatic performances in the 2001 annual report summary of the Royal Dutch/Shell Group of Companies, prepared by the accounting and auditing firms of KPMG and PricewatershouseCoopers. The title of this annual report summary is, significantly, *People, planet and profits*. Why is this title significant here? Because 'people', 'planet' and 'profits' correspond directly to the annual report's three main sections, which respectively are 'social performance', 'environmental performance' and 'economic performance'. In short, the entire annual activity of this major multinational corporation is presented and assessed for its stakeholders – and for the world at large – in terms of the integration of three different types of performance: social, environmental and economic.[16]

Royal Dutch/Shell's attempt to integrate multi-paradigmatic performances exemplifies the nature and functioning of performativity's operation at a global level. First, performativity is not 'one thing'; rather, it consists of many conflicting and, at times, contradictory performativities: cultural, organizational, technological, governmental, financial, environmental.[17] Second, the performance stratum functions precisely through ongoing attempts to negotiate multiple and competing performativities. While Lyotard stressed performativity as optimization or the maximizing of efficiency, performativity can be better understood as 'satisficing', first theorized by Herbert Simon.[18] Efficiency may often need to be compromised with other values, such as social efficacy or technological effectiveness. Decision-makers thus seek to satisfy competing demands, but because they work with limited knowledge, they must also make sacrifices; hence they *satisfice*, making not the best or optimum decision but one that is 'good enough'.

Likewise, global performativity operates through what we might call *satisficial rituals*, routinized performance review programs that consist of highly formalized attempts to measure, evaluate and improve different types of performance. Such evaluative programs are in no way limited to Royal Dutch/Shell. Quite the contrary: the focus on studying, evaluating and integrating social, environmental and economic performances is becoming increasingly important to companies and countries who dedicate themselves to sustainable development. Using guidelines established by the Global Reporting Initiative (GRI), some 323 organizations in 31 countries use social, environmental and economic performance measures to assess the impact their activities have on the natural environment and the social well-being of their workers, customers and communities. These organizations include small and large companies, governments and non-governmental organizations (NGOs). Now an independent organization itself, the GRI was founded in 1997 by the Coalition for Environmentally Responsible Economies and is an official collaborating centre of the United Nations Environment Programme.

We can sense the breadth of global performativity by turning to Global Compact Performance Model developed by the United Nations. In 1999, Secretary-General Kofi Annan announced an initiative aimed at encouraging private companies to work toward sustainable and inclusive global economic development. The Global Compact focuses on three main areas of concern: human rights, labour standards and the environment. The program became operational in 2000 and is today composed of a network of five agencies. Coordinated by the Global Compact Office, it includes the Office of the High Commissioner for Human Rights, the United Nations Environment Programme, the International Labour Organization, the United Nations Development Programme and the United Nations Industrial Development Organization. Currently, over 1,130 companies from 59 nations participate in the Global Compact. At the heart of the program is the goal of encouraging private companies to incorporate human rights, labour and environmental standards into their strategic planning and production processes. To this end, in 2002, a Global Compact Policy Dialog consisting of UN representatives, business practitioners, and labour and civil society organizations developed a Global Compact Performance Model:

> By *model*, we mean a system of rules, practices and means to achieve a set of results. By *performance* we mean a minimum of inputs and efforts to achieve the best results in the shortest period of time. In other words this [performance model] describes a blueprint or road map to help business to embrace the Global Compact principles and move toward a satisfactory performance without detracting from their other business goals.[19]

Here, the dialogue group defines performance at the most general level as minimizing inputs and optimizing outputs in a timely manner. Such 'minimaxing' of input/output recalls Lyotard's concept of performative optimization. At the same time, to achieve the Global Compact's criteria of 'satisfactory performance', companies must negotiate between traditional business performance measures (those of organizational and financial performance) and new, emerging performance measures (environmental and social performance, or human rights and fair labour practices). Such negotiations can be understood as satisficing rather than optimization.

The Global Reporting Initiative and the UN's Global Compact provide ample evidence of how performativity is going global and, indeed, in doing so they also reveal a final characteristic of global performativity. Performativity today operates through a complex network of social institutions, working not only at the level of nation-states, but also above them at the level of inter- and transnational organizations, such as the UN and the GRI, and below them, through businesses and NGOs. It is precisely this global networking of institutions that helps distinguish the performance stratum from the much more hierarchical and nationally-based institutions found on the disciplinary formation described by Foucault.

Conclusion

If performance describes a new epochal formation, it provides a context for understanding the complexities of audit culture. And it can, I hope, help us to think about the colliding financial, organizational, educational and cultural imperatives that shape contemporary education. But while it is important to recognize how universities around the world have been affected by financial and, more importantly, organizational forms of performance, it is also worth stressing that a wide variety of organizations have sought to incorporate educational processes into their own operation. Corporations such as Microsoft, for instance, have drawn on the university model to transform their business headquarters into 'corporate campuses', thereby stressing the challenging, educational and youth-oriented aspects of working there. At the same time, organizational development proponents seek to create 'learning organizations', institutions that not only train and educate individuals but also strive to learn *as* organizations: systems thinking, change management and total quality management strategies all stress collective and systemic learning and have been implemented in businesses, non-profit organizations and hospitals. Such developments point to the blurring of institutional borders that persistently characterizes performativity. In addition, they also point to the normative function that creativity, experimentation and diversity may paradoxically play. To survive, organizations must continually test their internal processes as well as their external borders and thus may actively encourage deviations, transgressions and differences that would have been intolerable within disciplinary institutions. Not all such diversity will be accepted, of course, but without some element of difference, organizations could not respond to changes in their environment or within themselves. Performativity, like the audit culture through which it operates, demands and produces high performance schooling.

Notes

[1] F. Allan Hanson, *Testing Testing: Social Consequences of the Examined Life* (Berkeley: University of California Press, 2000), p.1.

[2] Marilyn Strathern, 'Introduction: New accountabilities', in Marilyn Strathern [ed], *Audit Cultures: Anthropological studies in audit, ethics, and the academy* (London: Routledge, 2000), p.2.

[3] Max Weber, *From Max Weber: Essays in Sociology*, trans. H. H. Gerth and C. Wright Mills [eds] (New York: Oxford University Press, 1946), p.241.

[4] Strathern, 'Introduction', p.3.

[5] I have rehearsed this general theory more fully in Jon McKenzie, *Perform or Else: From Discipline to Performance* (London: Routledge, 2001).

[6] Jean-François Lyotard, *The Postmodern Condition*, trans. Geoff Bennington and Brian Massumi (Minneapolis: University of Minnesota Press, 1979), p.xxiv [emphasis added].

[7] Roberts, 'Rereading Lyotard: Knowledge, Commodification and Higher Education', *Electronic Journal of Sociology* (1998), http://www.sociology.org/content/vol003.003/roberts.html.

[8] Roberts, 'Rereading Lyotard'.

[9] Robin Usher and Nicky Solomon, 'Disturbing the Ivory Tower? Educational Research as Performance and Performativity', paper prepared for the Australian Association for Research in Education, 1998 Annual Conference, http://www.aare.edu.au/98pap/sol98172.htm.

[10] Usher and Solomon, 'Disturbing the Ivory Tower?'

[11] Financial Accounting Standards Board, 'Discussion Questions: FASB Task Force Meeting on Financial Performance Reporting by Business Enterprises', www.fasb.org/project/discussion_paper.pdf.

[12] See Susan Stanford Friedman, '"Border Talk", Hybridity, and Performativity', *Eurozine* (July 6, 2002), http://www.eurozine.com/article/2002-06-07-friedman-en.html#fn1.

[13] Robert G. Eccles, 'The Performance Measurement Manifesto', *Harvard Business Review on Measuring Corporate Performance* (Cambridge: Harvard Business School Press, 2003), p.25.

[14] Evelyn Eichel and Henry E. Bender, *Performance Appraisal: A Study of Current Techniques* (New York: American Management Association Research and Information Service, 1984), pp.11–12.

[15] See McKenzie, *Perform or Else*.

[16] See *People, planet and profits: The Shell Report 2001 Summary* (Royal Dutch Petroleum Company and The 'Shell' Transport and Trading Company, p.l.c., 2002).

[17] And the list need not stop here: there are still other paradigms of performance research, including educational, physiological, psychological, sexual and pharmaceutical paradigms.

[18] See Herbert A. Simon, *Models of Man* (New York: John Wiley and Sons, 1957).

[19] See 'A Company Performance Model for Achieving the Global Compact Principles', http://www.uneptie.org/outreach/compact/docs/GC-Dialogue2002-Model.pdf.

Jon McKenzie is Assistant Professor of English at Dartmouth College, USA. His publications include *Perform or Else: From Discipline to Performance* (Routledge, 2001), which will be translated and published in Croatian in 2004. His essays have appeared in the journals *The Drama Review*, *Frakcija*, and *Lusitania* and the anthologies *The Performance Studies Reader* and *Performance: Critical Concepts in Literary and Cultural Studies*.

parallax, 2004, vol. 10, no. 2, 63–72

Culture and Management

Zygmunt Bauman

The idea of 'culture' was coined and named in the third quarter of the 18th Century, as a shorthand term for the management of human thought and behaviour. 'Culture' was not born as a descriptive term, a summary name for the already achieved, observed and recorded regularities of the population-wide conduct (that use of the word 'culture' arrived about a century later, when the culture managers looked back on what they already came to view as their creation and following the world-creating God's example declared it to be good. 'Culture' came to mean the way one type of 'normatively regulated', regular human conduct differed from another type, under different management) – but as a declaration of *intent*.

The term 'culture' entered vocabulary as a name of *purposeful* activity. At the threshold of the modern era men and women, no longer accepted as 'brute facts', as links in the chain of Divine (i.e. non-negotiable and not-to-be-meddled-with) creation, indispensable even if mean, paltry and leaving much to be desired, came to be seen as both pliable and in dire need of repair and/or improvement. The term 'culture' was conceived inside the family of concepts that included terms like 'cultivation', 'husbandry', 'breeding' – all meaning improvement, prevention of impairment, arresting deterioration. What the farmer did to the seed through attentive care all the way from a seedling to the crop, could and ought to be done to the incipient human beings by education and training. Humans were not *born*, but *made*. They needed yet to *become* human – and in the course of becoming human (a trajectory which they would not negotiate if left to themselves) they had to be guided by other humans, educated and trained in the art of educating and training humans.

'Culture' appeared in vocabulary less than a hundred years *after* another crucial modern concept – of 'managing', meaning according to OED 'to cause (persons, animals etc.) to submit to one's control', 'to operate upon', 'to succeed in accomplishing' – and more than a hundred years *earlier* than another, synthesizing sense of 'management': 'to contrive to get along or pull through'. To manage, in a nutshell, meant to get things done in a way onto which they would not move on their own; to *re*-direct events according to one's design and will. To put it yet another way: to manage (to get control over the flow of events) came to mean the manipulation of probabilities – making certain conduct (openings or responses) of 'persons, animals etc.' more likely to take place than it would otherwise have done, while making some other moves utterly unlikely to happen. In the last account, to manage means to limit the freedom of the managed.

parallax
ISSN 1353-4645 print/ISSN 1460-700X online © 2004 Taylor & Francis Ltd
http://www.tandf.co.uk/journals
DOI: 10.1080/1353464042000208521

Just like '*agri*culture' is the vision of the field as seen from the perspective of the farmer, 'culture' metaphorically applied to humans was the vision of the social world as viewed through the eyes of the 'farmers of the human-growing fields' – the managers. The postulate or presumption of management was not a later addition and external intrusion: it has been from the beginning and throughout its history endemic to the concept. Deep in the heart of the 'culture' concept lies the premonition or tacit acceptance of an unequal, asymmetrical social relation – the split between acting and bearing the impact of action, between the managers and the managed, the knowing and the ignorant, the refined and the crude.

Theodor Wiesegrund Adorno points out that the 'inclusion of the objective spirit of an age in the single word "culture" betrays from the onset the administrative view, the task of which, looking down from on high, is to assemble, distribute, evaluate and organize'.[1] And he unpacks the defining traits of that spirit: 'The demand made by administration upon culture is essentially heteronomous: culture – no matter what form it takes – is to be measured by norms not inherent to it and which have nothing to do with the quality of the object, but rather with some type of abstract standards imposed from without [...]'.[2] As one could only expect in the case of an asymmetrical social relation, a quite different sight opens to the eyes scanning the relationship from the opposite, receiving end: (in other words, to the eyes of the 'managed') and a quite different evaluation is voiced (if people assigned to that end acquire a voice): the sight of an unwarranted and uncalled-for repression, and the verdict of illegitimacy and injustice. In that other version of the relationship's story, culture appears to be 'opposed to administration', since, as Oscar Wilde put it (provocatively, in Adorno's opinion) – culture is useless (or so it appears as long as the managers hold the monopoly on drawing the line separating use from waste); it represents the claims of the particular against the homogenizing pressure of the general, and it 'involves an irrevocably critical impulse towards the status quo and all institutions thereof'.[3] The clash of the two narratives is inevitable. It can be neither prevented nor pacified once it comes into the open. The managers-managed relationship is intrinsically agonistic; the two sides pursue two opposite purposes and are able to cohabit solely in a conflict-ridden, battle-ready mode.

Adorno recognizes the inevitability of the conflict. But he also points out that the antagonists need each other; however inconvenient and unpleasant the state of overt or clandestine enmity may be, the greatest misfortune that might befall culture is a complete and finite victory over its antagonist: 'culture suffers damage when it is planned and administrated; if it is left to itself, however, everything cultural threatens not only to lose the possibility of effect, but its very existence as well'.[4] In these words, he restates the sad conclusion to which he arrived when working (with Max Horkheimer) on *Dialectics of Enlightenment*: that 'the history of the old religions and schools like that of the modern parties and revolutions' teaches that the price of survival is 'the transformation of ideas into domination'.[5] This lesson of history ought to be particularly diligently studied, absorbed and put into practice by professional 'culture creators' who carry the main burden of the transgressive propensity of culture, making it their consciously embraced vocation and practising critique and transgression as their own mode of being:

The appeal to the creators of culture to withdraw from the process of administration and keep distant from it has a hollow ring. Not only would this deprive them of the possibility of earning a living, but also of every effect, every contact between works of art and society, something which the work of greatest integrity cannot do without, if it is not to perish.[6]

The paradox, indeed. Or a vicious circle... Culture cannot live in peace with management, particularly with an obtrusive and insidious management, and most particularly with a management aimed at twisting the culture's exploring/experimenting urge so that it fits into the frame of rationality the managers have drawn. The management's plot against the endemic freedom of culture is a perpetual *casus belli*. On the other hand, however, culture creators need managers if they wish (as most of them, bent on 'improving the world', do) to be seen, heard, listened to and to stand a chance of seeing their task/project through to the completion. Otherwise they risk marginality, impotence and oblivion.

Culture creators have no choice but to live with that paradox. However loudly they protest the managers' pretensions and interference, they would seek a *modus co-vivendi* with administration or sink into irrelevance. They may choose between managements pursuing different purposes and trimming the liberty of cultural creation according to different designs – but certainly not between acceptance and rejection of administration. Not realistically, at any rate.

This is so because the paradox in question stems from the fact that all the mutual mud-slinging notwithstanding, culture creators and managers are bound to share the same household and partake of the same endeavour. Theirs is a *sibling rivalry*. They are both after the same target, sharing the same goal: to make the world different from what it is at the moment and/or from what it is likely to turn into if left alone. Both of them derive from the critique of the *status quo* (even is their declared purposes are to conserve it or to restore it to *status quo ante*). If they quarrel, it is not about whether the world should be an object of constant intervention or left rather to its own inner tendencies – but about the direction which the intervention should take. More often than not their strife is about who is to be in charge; to whom belongs, or ought to be given, the right to decide the direction, and to select the tools with which its pursuit is monitored as well as the measures by which its progress is assessed.

Hannah Arendt spotted flawlessly and spelled out the gist of the conflict:

> An object is cultural depending on the duration of its permanence: its durable character is opposed to its functional aspect, that aspect which would make it disappear from the phenomenal world through use and wear and tear [...] Culture finds itself under threat when all objects of the world, produced currently or in the past, are treated solely as functions of the vital social processes – as if they had no other reason but satisfaction of some need – and it does not matter whether the needs in question are elevated or base.[7]

Culture aims above the head of realities of the day. It is not concerned with whatever has been put on the daily agenda and defined as the imperative of the moment – at least it strives to transcend the limiting impact of so defined 'topicality' and struggles to free itself of its demands.

Being used/consumed on the spot and dissolving in the process of instantaneous consumption is neither the cultural product's destination nor the criterion of the cultural object's value. Arendt would say: culture is after *beauty* – and I suggest that she chose that name for culture's concerns because the idea of 'beauty' is the very epitome of an elusive target that defies rational/causal explanation, has no purpose nor a visible use, serves nothing and cannot legitimate itself by reference to any need already felt, defined and scheduled for gratification. An object is cultural in as far as it outlives any use that might have attended to its creation.

Such an image of culture differs sharply from the common opinion, until recently prevalent also in academic literature – which, on the contrary, casts culture among the homeostatic appliances preserving the monotonous reproduction of social reality, its *mêmeté* – protection and continuation of its sameness over time. The notion of culture common to the writings classified under the rubric of social science has been one of a stabilizing, routine-and-repetition begetting mechanism, an instrument of inertia – not at all the ferment that prevents social reality from standing still and forces it into perpetual self-transcendence as Adorno and Arendt would insist it cannot but be; an element of self-renewing order, rather than of its eternal disruption and overhaul. In orthodox anthropological descriptions (one society = one culture) 'culture' appears as an efficient tool of 'pattern maintenance', a handmaiden of 'social structure' – of a permanent distribution of behavioural probabilities retaining its shape over time and successfully fighting back all occasional breaches of norm, disruptions and deviations threatening to throw the 'system' out of its 'equilibrium'. This is, to be sure, an extrapolation and a utopian horizon of a properly managed (or, to recall Talcott Parsons's once ubiquitous phrase, 'principally coordinated') social totality, with the distribution of probabilities stable and tightly controlled by a set of homeostatic contraptions among which 'culture' is assigned the pride of place; a kind of totality inside which any deviant behaviour of human units is promptly spotted, isolated before irreparable harm is done and swiftly defused or eliminated. Inside that vision of the society as a self-equilibrating system (that is, remaining obstinately the same despite the pressures of counter-veiling forces) *'culture' stands for the managers' dream come true: for an effective resistance to change.* And this is how the role of culture used to be most commonly perceived still two-three decades ago.

Much has happened in those two-three decades, though. To start with, the 'managerial revolution mark two', conducted surreptitiously under the banner of 'neo–liberalism': managers switching from 'normative regulation' to 'seduction', from day-to-day policing to PR, and from the stolid, over-regulated, routine-based panoptical model of power to domination through diffuse uncertainty, *precarité* and a continuous though haphazard disruption of routine. And then, gradual dismantling of the state-serviced frame in which the paramount parts of life-politics used to be conducted, and the shifting/drifting of life politics onto the domain presided over by the consumer market that thrives on the frailty of routines and their rapid super-cession – rapid enough to prevent their hardening into habits or norms. In this new setting, there is little demand for the bridling and taming of a transgressive urge and of the compulsive experimentation dubbed 'culture' in order to harness it to the vehicles of self-equilibration and continuity. Or at least the orthodox carriers of that demand – managers of nation-building states – lost their interest in such harnessing, and the new script-writers and directors of cultural drama wish everything but tamed, regular, routine-bound, inflexible conduct of humans, transformed now into consumers first and last.

With the principal characters of the 'solid modernity' drama leaving the stage or reduced to the half-mute role of supernumeraries, and with their replacements reluctant to emerge from the wings, our contemporaries found themselves acting in what can be properly called, following Hannah Arendt, and through her, Bertold Brecht, 'dark times'. This is how Arendt unpacks the nature and the origins of that darkness:

> If it is the function of the public realm to throw light on the affairs of men by providing a space of appearances in which they can show in deed and word, for better and worse, who they are and what they can do, then darkness has come when this light is extinguished by a 'credibility gap' and 'invisible government', by speech that does not disclose what is but sweeps it under the carpet, by exhortations, moral or otherwise, that, under the pretext of upholding old truths, degrade all truth to meaningless triviality.[8]

And this is how she described its consequences:

> (T)he public realm has lost the power of illumination which was originally part of its nature. More and more people in the countries of the Western world, which since the decline of the ancient world has regarded freedom from politics as one of the basic freedoms, make use of this freedom and have retreated from the world and their obligations within it [...] But with each such retreat an almost demonstrable loss to the world takes place: what is lost is the specific and usually irreplaceable in-between which should have formed between the individual and his fellow men.[9]

Withdrawal from politics and the public realm will turn therefore, wrote Hannah Arendt prophetically, into the 'basic attitude of the modern individual, who in his alienation from the world can truly reveal himself only in privacy and in the intimacy of face-to face encounters'.[10]

It is that newly gained/enforced privacy and the 'intimacy of face-to-face encounters', the inseparable companion of 'dark times', that is serviced by the consumer market, promoting and thriving on the universal contingency of consumer life; capitalizing on the fluidity of social placements and frailty of human bonds, on the contentious and so unstable and unpredictable status of individual rights, obligations and commitments, and on the present lying beyond the grasp of its denizens and on the future endemically and incurably uncertain. Under pressure and out of impotence, yet with little resistance (if not willingly), the state managers abandon the ambition of normative regulation for which they once stood accused by Adorno and other critics of the emergent 'fully administered mass society' – putting themselves instead in the 'agentic state' and assuming the role of 'honest brokers' of the market's needs (read: demands).

Culture creators may still resent, and they do resent, the obtrusive intervention of the managers, who insist – true to the managers' habit – on measuring cultural performance by extrinsic criteria, alien to the irrational logic of cultural creativity, and use the power and resources they command to secure obedience to the rules they set. This principal objection to interference is not however, as it has been argued before, a novel departure – but just another chapter in a long story of 'sibling rivalry' with no end in sight: for better or worse, for better *and* worse, cultural creations need managers – lest they should die in the same ivory tower in which they had been conceived...

What is truly novel are the *criteria* which the present-day managers, in their new role of agents of the market forces rather than of the nation-building state powers, deploy to assess, 'audit', 'monitor', judge, censure, reward and punish their wards. Naturally, they are the consumer-market criteria, such as set preference for instant consumption, instant gratification and instant profit. A consumer market catering for long-term needs, not to mention eternity, would be a contradiction in terms. Consumer market propagates rapid circulation, shorter distance from use to waste and waste disposal, and immediate replacement of no longer profitable goods. All that stands in a jarring opposition to the nature of cultural creation. And so the novelty is the parting of ways of the siblings still engaged in rivalry. The stake of the new chapter of the age-long tug-of-war is not only the answer to the question 'who is in charge?', but the sheer substance of 'being in charge' – its purpose and its consequences. We may go a step (a small step, as it were) further and say that the stake is the survival of culture as we came to know it since the Altamira caves had been painted. Can culture survive the demise of infinity – that first 'collateral casualty' of the consumer market's triumph? The answer to that question is that we don't truly know – though we may have valid reasons to suspect a 'no' answer, and following Hans Jonas's advise to the denizens of the 'era of uncertainty' we may put more trust in the oracles of the 'prophets of doom'...

To subordinate cultural creativity to the criteria of the consumer market means to demand of cultural creations that they accept the prerequisite of all would-be consumer products: that they legitimize themselves in terms of market value (and their *current* market value, to be sure) or perish.

The first question addressed to cultural offers claiming validity and bidding for recognition is that of sufficient demand, supported with adequate capacity to pay. Let us note that consumer demand being notoriously capricious, freak and volatile, the records of consumer-market's rule over culture are full of mistaken prognoses, wide-of-the-mark evaluations and grossly incorrect decisions. In practice, that rule boils down to compensating the absent quality analysis with the overshooting of potential targets and the hedging of bets – in other words, with wasteful excess and excessive waste (G.B. Shaw, a dedicated amateur-photographer in addition to his play-writing, advised photographers to follow the example of codfish that must spawn a thousand eggs so that one mature codfish can be hatched; it seems that the whole consumer industry, and the marketing managers keeping it alive, follow Shaw's advise). Such a strategy may sometimes insure against the exorbitant losses caused by mistaken cost-effects analysis; it would however do little or nothing to assure that cultural products stand a chance of revealing their true quality when no market demand for them is in sight (an eminently *short* sight, given the endemic 'short-termism' of the calculations).

It is now the prospective clients, their numbers and the volume of cash at their disposal that decide (though unknowingly) the fate of cultural creations. The line dividing the 'successful' (and therefore commanding public attention) cultural products from failed cultural products (that is, unable to break through into notoriety) is drawn by sales, ratings and box-office returns (according to Daniel J. Boorstin's witty definitions, 'celebrity is a person who is known for his well-knownness', while 'a best seller' is a book which somehow sold well 'simply because it was selling well'.[11] Let me add that chequebook journalism would take care of the close link between the two rules). But there is no correlation that the theorists and critics of contemporary art managed to establish between the virtues of a cultural creation and its celebrity status. If a correlation is to be found, it will be found between celebrity status and the power of the brand that lifted the incipient *objet d'art* from obscurity into the limelight. The contemporary equivalent of good fortune or a stroke of luck is Charles Saatchi stopping his car in front of an obscure side-street shop selling bric-a-brac, dreamed/craved by the obscure side-street persons who made them, to be proclaimed works of art. They will turn into works of art, and overnight, once they are put on display in the gallery whose walls and entry gates separate the good art from bad, and art from non-art. The name of the gallery lends its glory to the names of the artists on exhibition. In the vexingly confusing world of flexible norms and floating values, this is – not unexpectedly – a universal trend. As Naomi Klein succinctly put it: 'many of today's best-known manufacturers no longer produce products and advertise them, but rather buy products and "brand" them'.[12] Brand and the logo attached (it is the shopping bag with the name of the gallery that gives meaning to the purchases inside) do not add value – they are value, the market value, and thus value as such.

It is not just the companies that lend value to products through branding (or devalue the products by withdrawing their logo). Perhaps the most potent brands are events: celebrated events, massively attended thanks to being known for their well-knownness and selling masses of tickets because of the tickets being known to sell well. 'Events' are better than the other brands counting on the loyalty of the faithful attuned to the notoriously short span of public memory and the cut-throat competition between allures vying for the consumers' attention. Events, like all *bona fide* consumer products, bear a 'use-by' date; their designers and supervisors may leave the long-term concerns out of their calculation (with a double benefit of huge savings and confidence-inspiring resonance with the spirit of the age), planning and catering for (to recall George Steiner's apt phrase) 'maximal impact and instant obsolescence'. Again, the (literally and metaphorically) spectacular career of the fixed-time event, as the most felicitous and ever more often employed form of branding, chimes well with the universal tendency of the liquid-modern setting. Cultural products – whether inanimate objects or educated humans, tend to be enlisted in the service of 'projects', admittedly one-off and short lived undertakings. And, as the research team quoted by Naomi Klein found out: 'you can indeed brand not only sand, but also wheat, beef, brick, metals; concrete, chemicals, corn grits and an endless variety of commodities, traditionally considered immune to the process',[13] that are believed (wrongly, as it transpires) to be able to stand on their own feet and prove their point just by unfolding and demonstrating their own excellence.

'Consumerist syndrome' applied to culture centres on an emphatic denial of the virtue of procrastination, of the 'delay of satisfaction' precept – those foundational principles of the 'society of producers' or 'productivist society'.

In the inherited hierarchy of recognized values, 'consumerist syndrome' has dethroned duration and elevated transience. It has put the value of novelty above that of the lasting. It has radically shortened the time-span separating not just the want from its fulfilment (as many observers, inspired or misled by credit agencies, suggested), but also the usefulness and desirability of possessions from their uselessness and rejection; the life-expectation of the 'fulfilling capacity' of acquisitions has fallen dramatically. Among the objects of human desire, 'consumerist syndrome' put appropriation (quickly followed by waste-disposal) in place of possessions. Among human preoccupations, it put the precautions against things (animate as much as inanimate) 'outstaying their welcome' well in front of the technique of 'holding fast', of staying put and of the long-term (not to mention interminable) engagement. It also shortened drastically the life-expectation of desire, the time distance from desire to its gratification and from gratification to the waste-disposal tip. Let me restate the point: 'consumerist syndrome' is all about speed, excess and waste; about precepts diametrically opposed to those guiding cultural creativity.

Of course, it would be as unjust as it is unwise to accuse the consumer industry, and consumer industry alone, of the plight in which cultural creation finds itself today. That industry is well geared to the form of life which I used to call 'liquid modernity'.[14] That industry and that form of life are attuned to each other and reinforce each other's grip on the choices men and women of our times may realistically make.

As the great Italian sociologist, Alberto Melucci, used to say – 'we are plagued by the fragility of the presentness which calls for a firm foundation where none exists'.[15] And so, 'when contemplating change, we are always torn between desire and fear, between anticipation and uncertainty'.[16] This is it: *uncertainty*. Or, as Ulrich Beck prefers to call it, the *risk*: that unwanted, awkward and vexing, but perpetual and un-detachable fellow-traveller (or a stalker rather?!) of all anticipation – a sinister spectre haunting the decision-makers that we all, whether we like it or not, are. For us, as Melucci pithily put it, 'choice became a destiny'.[17]

Indeed, everything around in the 'really existing world' seems to be but 'until further notice'. The allegedly rock-solid companies are unmasked as figments of accountants' imagination. Whatever is commended as 'meat for you' today may be reclassified tomorrow as poison. Apparently firm commitments and solemnly signed agreements may be overturned overnight. And promises, or most of them, seem to be made in order to be un-kept and betrayed. There seems to be no stable, secure island among the tides. To quote Melucci once more: 'we no longer possess a home; we are repeatedly called upon to build and then rebuild one, like the three little pigs of the fairy tale, or we have to carry it along with us on our backs like snails'.[18] To sum it all up: at no other time has Robert Louis Stevenson's memorable verdict 'to travel hopefully is a better thing than to arrive' sounded truer than it does in our floating and flowing, fluid modern world.

When destinations move or lose their charm faster than legs can walk, cars ride or planes fly, keeping on the move matters more than the destination. The question '*how* to do it' looks more important and urgent than the query '*what* to do'. Not to make a habit of anything practised at the moment, not to be tied up by the legacy of one's own past, wearing current identity as one wears shirts that can be replaced when falling out of use or out of fashion, rejecting past lessons and abandoning past skills with no inhibition or regret – are all becoming the hallmarks of the present-day, liquid-modern life politics and attributes of liquid-modern rationality. Liquid-modern culture feels no longer a culture of learning and accumulating like those cultures recorded in the historians' and ethnographers' reports. It looks instead a *culture of disengagement, discontinuity, and forgetting*.

That last phrase – is it not a contradiction in terms? This is the big question, perhaps the life-and-death question as far as culture is concerned. For centuries culture lived in an uneasy symbiosis with management, tussling uncomfortably, sometimes suffocating, in the managers' embrace – but also running to the managers for shelter and emerging reinvigorated and strengthened from the encounter. Would culture survive the change of management? Won't it be allowed anything but a butterfly-like, ephemeral existence? Won't the new management, true to the new management style, limit its wardenship to asset-stripping? Won't the cemetery of deceased or aborted 'cultural events' replace the rising slope as a fitful metaphor of culture?

William de Kooning suggests that in this world of ours 'content is a glimpse', a fugitive vision, a look in passing.[19] While a most incisive analyst of the twists and turns of postmodern and post-postmodern culture, Yves Michaud suggests that aesthetics, culture's forever elusive and stubbornly pursued target, is these days consumed and celebrated in a world emptied, and void, of the works of art[20]...

Notes

[1] Theodor W. Adorno, 'Culture and Administration', trans. Wes Blomster, in J.M. Bernstein [ed], *The Culture Industry: Selected essays on Mass Culture by Theodor W. Adorno* (London: Routledge, 1991), p.93. Let me point out that the word 'management' better than 'administration' conveys the gist of the German term *Verwaltung* used in the original.

[2] Adorno, 'Culture and Administration', p.98.
[3] Adorno, 'Culture and Administration', pp.93, 98, 100.
[4] Adorno, 'Culture and Administration', p.94.
[5] Theodor Adorno and Max Horkheimer, *Dialectics of Enlightenment*, trans. John Cumming (London: Verso, 1979), pp.216–7.

[6] Adorno, 'Culture and Administration', p.103.

[7] Hannah Arendt, *La crise de la culture* (Paris: Gallimard, 1968), pp.266–7.

[8] Hannah Arendt, *Men in Dark Times* (New York: Harcourt Brace & Company, 1983), p.VIII.

[9] Arendt, *Men in Dark Times*, pp.4–5.

[10] Arendt, *Men in Dark Times*, p.24.

[11] Daniel J. Boorstin, *The Image: A Guide to Pseudo-Events in America* (New York: Atheneum, 1962), p.61.

[12] Naomi Klein, *No Logo* (London: Flamingo, 2001), p.5.

[13] Klein, *No Logo*, p.25.

[14] Zygmunt Bauman, *Liquid Modernity* (Cambridge: Polity Press, 2000).

[15] See Alberto Melucci, *The Playing Self: Person and Meaning in the Planetary Society* (Cambridge: Cambridge University Press, 1996), pp.43ff. This is an extended version of the Italian original published in 1991 under the title *Il gioco dell'io*.

[16] Melucci, *The Playing Self*, p.43.

[17] Melucci, *The Playing Self*, p.43.

[18] Melucci, *The Playing Self*, p.43.

[19] W. De Kooning, *Écrits et propos* (Paris: Éditions de l'Ensb-a, 1992), pp.90ff.

[20] Yves Michaud, *L'art à l'état gazeux* (Paris: Stock, 2003), p.9.

Zygmunt Bauman is Emeritus professor of sociology at the Universities of Leeds and Warsaw. His latest publications include *Liquid Love* (2003) and *Wasted Lives* (2004).

parallax, 2004, vol. 10, no. 2, 73–89

Cultural Studies and the Politics of Public Pedagogy: Making the Political More Pedagogical

Henry A. Giroux

Neoliberalism as Public Pedagogy

> Our age is the time of 'individual utopias', of utopias privatized, and so it comes naturally (as well as being a fashionable thing to do) to deride and ridicule such projects which imply a revision of the options which are collectively put at the disposal of individuals.[1]

The ascendancy of neoliberal corporate culture into every aspect of American life both consolidates economic power in the hands of the few and aggressively attempts to break the power of unions, decouple income from productivity, subordinate the needs of society to the market, and deem public services and goods an unconscionable luxury. But it does more. It thrives on a culture of cynicism, insecurity and despair. Conscripts in a relentless campaign for personal responsibility, Americans are now convinced that they have little to hope for – and gain from – the government, non-profit public spheres, democratic associations, public and higher education, or other non-governmental social forces. With few exceptions, the project of democratizing public goods has fallen into disrepute in the popular imagination as the logic of the market undermines the most basic social solidarities. The consequences include not only a weakened state, but a growing sense of insecurity, cynicism and political retreat on the part of the general public. The incessant calls for self-reliance that now dominate public discourse betray a hollowed out and refigured state that neither provides adequate safety nets for its populace, especially those who are young, poor or marginalized, nor gives any indication that it will serve the interests of its citizens in spite of constitutional guarantees. In short, private interests trump social needs, and economic growth becomes more important than social justice.

Defined as the paragon of modern social relations by Friedrich A. von Hayek, Milton Friedman, Robert Nozick, Francis Fukuyama and other market fundamentalists, neoliberalism attempts to eliminate an engaged critique about its most basic principles and social consequences by embracing the 'market as the arbiter of social destiny'.[2] Not only does neoliberalism empty the public treasury, hollow out public services, limit the vocabulary and imagery available to recognize anti-democratic forms of power, and narrow models of individual agency, it also undermines the critical functions of any viable democracy by undercutting the ability of individuals to engage

parallax
ISSN 1353-4645 print/ISSN 1460-700X online © 2004 Taylor & Francis Ltd
http://www.tandf.co.uk/journals
DOI: 10.1080/1353464042000208530

in the continuous translation between public considerations and private interests by collapsing the public into the realm of the private. As Bauman observes, 'It is no longer true that the "public" is set on colonizing the "private". The opposite is the case: it is the private that colonizes the public space, squeezing out and chasing away everything which cannot be fully, without residue, translated into the vocabulary of private interests and pursuits'.[3] Divested of its political possibilities and social underpinnings, freedom offers few opportunities for people to translate private worries into public concerns and collective struggle.[4]

Within neoliberalism's market-driven discourse, corporate power marks the space of a new kind of public pedagogy, one in which the production, dissemination and circulation of ideas emerges from the educational force of the larger culture. Public pedagogy in this sense refers to a powerful ensemble of ideological and institutional forces whose aim is to produce competitive, self-interested individuals vying for their own material and ideological gain. Corporate public pedagogy culture largely cancels out or devalues gender, class-specific and racial injustices of the existing social order by absorbing the democratic impulses and practices of civil society within narrow economic relations. Corporate public pedagogy has become an all-encompassing cultural horizon for producing market identities, values and practices.

For example, some neoliberal advocates argue that the answer to solving the health care and education crises faced by many states can be fixed by selling off public assets to private interests. The Pentagon even considered, if only for a short time, turning the war on terror and security concerns over to futures markets, subject to on-line trading. Thus, non-commodified public spheres are replaced by commercial spheres as the substance of critical democracy is emptied out and replaced by a democracy of goods available to those with purchasing power and the increasing expansion of the cultural and political power of corporations throughout the world.

Under neoliberalism, dominant public pedagogy with its narrow and imposed schemes of classification and limited modes of identification uses the educational force of the culture to negate the basic conditions for critical agency. As Pierre Bourdieu has pointed out, political action is only 'possible because agents, who are part of the social world, have knowledge of this world and because one can act on the social world by acting on their knowledge of this world'.[5] Politics often begins when it becomes possible to make power visible, to challenge the ideological circuitry of hegemonic knowledge, and to recognize that 'political subversion presupposes cognitive subversion, a conversion of the vision of the world'.[6] But another element of politics focuses on where politics happens, how proliferating sites of pedagogy bring into being new forms of resistance, raise new questions, and necessitate alternative visions regarding autonomy and the possibility of democracy itself.

What is crucial to recognize in the work of theorists such as Raymond Williams, Stuart Hall, Pierre Bourdieu, Noam Chomsky, Robert McChesney and others is that neoliberalism is more than an economic theory; it also constitutes the conditions for a radically refigured cultural politics. That is, it provides, to use Raymond Williams's term, a new mode of 'permanent education' in which dominant sites of pedagogy engage in diverse forms of pedagogical address to put into play a limited range of identities, ideologies and subject positions that both reinforce neoliberal social relations and undermine the possibility for democratic politics.[7] The economist William Greider goes so far as to argue that the diverse advocates of neoliberalism currently in control of the American government want to 'roll back the twentieth century literally'[8] by establishing the priority of private institutions and market identities, values and relationships as the organizing principles of public life. This is a discourse that wants to squeeze out ambiguity from public space, dismantle the social provisions and guarantees provided by the welfare state, and eliminate democratic politics by making the notion of the social impossible to imagine beyond the isolated consumer and the logic of the market.[9] The ideological essence of this new public pedagogy is well expressed by Grover Norquist, the president of the Americans for Tax Reform and arguably Washington's leading right-wing strategist, who argues that 'My goal is to cut government in half in twenty-five years, to get it down to the size where we can drown it in the bathtub'.[10]

These new sites of public pedagogy which have become the organizing force of neoliberal ideology are not restricted to schools, blackboards and test taking. Nor do they incorporate the limited forms of address found in schools. Such sites operate within a wide variety of social institutions and formats including sports and entertainment media, cable television networks, churches and channels of elite and popular culture such as advertising. Profound transformations have taken place in the public space, producing new sites of pedagogy marked by a distinctive confluence of new digital and media technologies, growing concentrations of corporate power, and unparalleled meaning producing capacities. Unlike traditional forms of pedagogy, knowledge and desire are inextricably connected to modes of pedagogical address mediated through unprecedented electronic technologies that include high speed computers, new types of digitized film and CD-ROMs. The result is a public pedagogy that plays a decisive role in producing a diverse cultural sphere that gives new meaning to education as a political force. What is surprising about the cultural politics of neoliberalism is that cultural studies theorists have either ignored or largely underestimated the symbolic and pedagogical dimensions of the struggle that neoliberal corporate power has put into place for the last thirty years, particularly under the ruthless administration of George W. Bush.

Making the Pedagogical More Political

> The need for permanent education, in our changing society, will be met in one way or another. It is now on the whole being met, though with many valuable exceptions and efforts against the tide, by an integration of this teaching with the priorities and interests of a capitalist society, and of a capitalist society, moreover, which necessarily retains as its central principle the idea of a few governing, communicating with and teaching the many.[11]

At this point in American history, neoliberal capitalism is not simply too overpowering; on the contrary, 'democracy is too weak'.[12] Hence, the increasing influence of money over politics, corporate interests overriding public concerns, and the growing tyranny of unchecked corporate power and avarice. Culture combines with politics to turn struggles over power into entertainment, as is the case in the California recall of Governor Davis and the election of Arnold Schwarzenegger as the new occupant of the Governor's office. But more importantly, under neoliberalism, pedagogy has become thoroughly politicized in reactionary terms as it constructs knowledge, values and identities through a dominant media that has become a handmaiden of corporate power. For instance, soon after the invasion of Iraq, *The New York Times* released a survey indicating that 42 percent of the American public believed that Saddam Hussein was directly responsible for the September 11 attacks on the World Trade Center and the Pentagon. CBS also released a news poll indicating that 55 percent of the public believed that Saddam Hussein directly supported the terrorist organization *Al Qaeda*. A majority of Americans also believed that Saddam Hussein had weapons of mass destruction, was about to build a nuclear bomb, and that he would unleash it eventually on an unsuspecting American public. None of these claims had any basis in fact since no evidence existed to even remotely confirm that any of these assertions were true. Of course, these opinions held by a substantial number of Americans did not simply fall from the sky, they were ardently legitimated by President Bush, Vice President Cheney, Colin Powell and Condolezza Rice, while daily reproduced uncritically in all of the dominant media. These misrepresentations and strategic distortions circulated in the dominant press either with uncritical, jingoistic enthusiasm, as in the case of the Fox News Channel, or through the dominant media's refusal to challenge such claims – both positions, of course, in opposition to foreign news sources such as the BBC which repeatedly challenged such assertions. Such deceptions are never innocent and in this case appear to have been shamelessly used by the Bush administration to both muster support for the Iraqi invasion and an ideologically driven agenda 'that overwhelmingly favors the president's wealthy supporters and is driving the federal government toward a long-term fiscal catastrophe'.[13]

While not downplaying the seriousness of government deception, I believe there is another serious issue that underlines these events in which the most important casualty is not simply the integrity of the Bush administration, but democracy itself. One of the central legacies of modern democracy, with its roots in the Enlightenment classical liberal tradition, and most evident in the twentieth century in work as diverse as W.E.B. Du Bois, Raymond Williams, Cornelius Castoriadis, John Dewey and Paulo Freire among others, is the important recognition that a substantive democracy cannot exist without educated citizens. For some, the fear of democracy itself translated into an attack on a truly public and accessible education for all citizens. For others such as the progressive Walter Lippman, who wrote extensively on democracy in the 1920s, it meant creating two modes of education. One mode for the elite who would rule the country and be the true participants in the democratic process and the other branch of education for the masses, whose education would train them to be spectators rather than participants in shaping democratic public life. Du Bois recognized that such a bifurcation of educational opportunity was increasingly becoming a matter of commonsense, but rejected it outright.[14] Similarly, in opposition, to the enemies of democracy and the elitists, radical social critics such as Cornelius Castoriadis, Paulo Freire, Stuart Hall and others believed that education for a democratic citizenry was an essential condition of equality and social justice and had to be provided through public, higher, popular and adult education.

While Castoriadis and others were right about linking education and democracy, they had no way in their time of recognizing that the larger culture would extend, if not supersede, institutionalized education as the most important educational force in the developed societies. In fact, education and pedagogy have been synonymous with schooling in the public mind. Challenging such a recognition does not invalidate the importance of formal education to democracy, but it does require a critical understanding of how the work of education takes place in a range of other spheres such as advertising, television, film, the Internet, video games and the popular press. Rather than invalidate the importance of schooling, it extends the sites of pedagogy and in doing so broadens and deepens the meaning of cultural pedagogy. The concept of public pedagogy also underscores the central importance of formal spheres of learning that unlike their popular counterparts – driven largely by commercial interests that more often mis-educate the public – must provide citizens with those critical capacities, modes of literacies, knowledge and skills that enable them to both read the world critically and participate in shaping and governing it. Pedagogy at the popular level must now be a central concern of formal schooling itself. I am not claiming that public or higher education are free from corporate influence and dominant ideologies, but that such models of education, at best, provide the spaces and conditions for prioritizing civic values over commercial interests (i.e. it self-consciously educates future citizens capable of participating in and reproducing a democratic society). In spite of their present embattled status and contradictory roles, institutional schooling remains uniquely placed to prepare students to both understand and influence the larger educational forces that shape their lives. Such institutions along with their cultural studies advocates by virtue of their privileged position and dedication to freedom and democracy also have an obligation to draw upon those traditions and resources capable of providing a critical and humanistic education to all students in order to prepare them for a world in which information and power have taken on a new and powerful dimension. One entry into this challenge is to address the contributions that cultural studies and critical pedagogy have made in the last few decades to such issues, particularly with respect to how the relationship between culture and power constitutes a new site of both politics and pedagogy.

Cultural Studies and the Question of Pedagogy

> City walls, books, spectacles, events educate – yet now they mostly *miseducate* their residents. Compare the lessons, taken by the citizens of Athens (women and slaves included), during the performances of Greek tragedies with the kind of knowledge which is today consumed by the spectator of *Dynasty* or *Perdue de vue*.[15]

My own interest in cultural studies emerges out of an ongoing project to theorize the regulatory and emancipatory relationship among culture, power and politics as expressed through the dynamics of what can be called public pedagogy. This project concerns, in part, the diverse ways in which culture functions as a contested sphere over the production, distribution and regulation of power and how and where it operates both symbolically and institutionally as an educational, political and economic force. Drawing upon a long tradition in cultural studies work, culture is viewed as constitutive and political, not only reflecting larger forces but also constructing them; in this instance, culture not only mediates history, it shapes it. In this formulation, power is a central element of culture just as culture is a crucial element of power.[16] As Bauman observes, 'Culture is a permanent revolution of sorts. To say "culture" is to make another attempt to account for the fact that the human world (the world moulded by the humans and the world which moulds humans) is perpetually, unavoidably – and unremediably *noch nicht geworden* (not-yet-accomplished), as Ernst Bloch beautifully put it'.[17]

I am suggesting that culture is a crucial terrain for theorizing and realizing the political as an articulation and intervention into the social, a space in which politics is pluralized, recognized as contingent, and open to many formations.[18] But culture is also a crucial sphere for articulating the dialectical and mutually constitutive dynamics between the global political circuits that now frame material relations of power and a cultural politics in which matters of representation and meaning shape and offer concrete examples of how politics is expressed, lived and experienced through the modalities of daily existence. Culture, in this instance, is the ground of both contestation and accommodation and it is increasingly characterized by the rise of mega corporations and new technologies which are transforming radically the traditional spheres of the economy, industry, society and everyday life. I am referring not only to the development of new information technologies but also the enormous concentration of ownership and power among a limited number of corporations that now control the diverse number of media technologies and markets.[19] Culture now plays a central role in producing narratives, metaphors, images and desiring maps that exercise a powerful pedagogical force over how people think about themselves and their relationship to others. From this perspective, culture is the primary sphere in which individuals, groups and institutions engage in the art of translating the diverse and multiple relations that mediate between private life and public concerns. It is also the sphere in which the translating and pedagogical possibilities of culture are under assault, particularly as the forces of neoliberalism dissolves public issues into utterly privatized and individualistic concerns.[20]

Against the neoliberal attack on all things social, culture must be defended as the site where exchange and dialogue become crucial as an affirmation of a democratically configured space of the social in which the political is actually taken up and lived out through a variety of intimate relations and social formations. Far from being exclusively about matters of representation and texts, culture becomes a site, event and performance in which identities and modes of agency are configured through the mutually determined forces of thought and action, body and mind, and time and space. Culture is the public space where common matters, shared solidarities and public engagements provide the fundamental elements of democracy. Culture is also the pedagogical and political ground in which shared solidarities and a global public sphere can be imagined as a condition of democratic possibilities. Culture offers a common space in which to address the radical demand of a pedagogy that allows critical discourse to confront the inequities of power and promote the possibilities of shared dialogue and democratic transformation. Culture affirms the social as a fundamentally political space just as it attempts within the current historical moment to deny its relevance and its centrality as a political necessity. And culture's urgency, as

Nick Couldry observes, resides in its possibilities for linking politics to matters of individual and social agency as they are lived out in particular democratic spheres, institutional forms and communities in process. He writes:

> For what is urgent now is not defending the full range of cultural production and consumption from elitist judgement but defending the possibility of any shared site for an emergent democratic politics. The contemporary mission of cultural studies, if it has one, lies not with the study of 'culture' (already a cliché of management and marketing manuals), but with the fate of a '*common* culture,' and its contemporary deformations.[21]

Central to any viable notion of cultural studies is the primacy of culture and power, organized through an understanding of how the political becomes pedagogical, particularly in terms of how private issues are connected to larger social conditions and collective forces; that is, how the very processes of learning constitute the political mechanisms through which identities are shaped, desires mobilized, and experiences take on form and meaning within those collective conditions and larger forces that constitute the realm of the social. In this context, pedagogy is no longer restricted to what goes on in schools, but becomes a defining principle of a wide ranging set of cultural apparatuses engaged in what Raymond Williams has called 'permanent education'. Williams rightfully believed that education in the broadest sense plays a central role in any viable form of cultural politics. He writes:

> What [permanent education] valuably stresses is the educational force of our whole social and cultural experience. It is therefore concerned, not only with continuing education, of a formal or informal kind, but with what the whole environment, its institutions and relationships, actively and profoundly teaches [...] [Permanent education also refers to] the field in which our ideas of the world, of ourselves and of our possibilities, are most widely and often most powerfully formed and disseminated. To work for the recovery of control in this field is then, under any pressures, a priority.[22]

Williams argued that any viable notion of critical politics would have to pay closer 'attention to the complex ways in which individuals are formed by the institutions to which they belong, and in which, by reaction, the institutions took on the color of individuals thus formed'.[23] Williams also foregrounded the crucial political question of how agency unfolds within a variety of cultural spaces structured within unequal relations of power.[24] He was particularly concerned about the connections between pedagogy and political agency, especially in light of the emergence of a range of new technologies that greatly proliferated the amount of information available to people while at the same time constricting the substance and ways in which such meanings entered the public domain. The realm of culture for Williams took on a new role in the latter part of the twentieth century because the actuality of economic power and its attendant networks of pedagogical control now exercised more influence than ever before in shaping how identities are produced, desires mobilized and everyday sociality acquired the force of common sense.[25] Williams clearly understood that making the political more pedagogical meant recognizing that where and how the psyche locates itself in public discourse, visions and passions provide the groundwork for agents to enunciate, act and reflect on themselves and their relations to others and the wider social order.

Unfortunately, Williams emphasis on making the pedagogical more political has not occupied a central place in the work of most cultural studies theorists. Pedagogy in most cultural studies accounts is either limited to the realm of schooling, dismissed as a discipline with very little academic cultural capital, or is rendered reactionary through the claim that it simply accommodates the paralyzing grip of governmental institutions that normalize all pedagogical practices. Within this discourse, pedagogy largely functions to both normalize relations of power and overemphasize agency at the expense of institutional pressures, embracing what Tony Bennett calls 'all agency and no structure'.[26] This criticism, however, does little to explore or highlight the complicated, contradictory and determining ways in which the institutional pressures of schools (and other pedagogical sites) and the social capacities of educators are mediated within unequal relations of power. Instead, Bennett simply reverses the formula and buttresses his own notion of governmentality as a theory of structures without agents. Of course, this position also ignores the role of various sites of pedagogy and the operational work they perform in producing knowledge, values, identities and subject positions. But more importantly it reflects the more general refusal on the part of many cultural studies theorists to take up the relationship between pedagogy and agency, on the one hand, and the relationship between the crisis of culture, education and democracy on the other. Given such a myopic vision, left leaning intellectuals who are dismissive of formal education sites have no doubt made it easier for the more corporate and entrepreneurial interests to dominate colleges and universities.

Unfortunately, many cultural studies theorists have failed to take seriously Antonio Gramsci's insight that '[e]very relationship of "hegemony" is necessarily an educational relationship' – with its implication that education as a cultural pedagogical practice takes place across multiple sites as it signals how, within diverse contexts, education makes us both subjects of and subject to relations of power.[27] I want to build on Gramsci's insight by exploring in greater detail the connection among democracy, political agency and pedagogy by analyzing some of the work of the late, French philosopher, Cornelius Castoriadis. Castoriadis has made seminal, and often overlooked, contributions to the role of pedagogy and its centrality to political democracy. I focus on this radical tradition in order to reclaim a legacy of critical thinking that refuses to decouple education from democracy, politics from pedagogy, and understanding from public intervention. This tradition of critical thought signals for educators and cultural studies advocates the importance of investing in the political as part of a broader effort to revitalize notions of democratic citizenship, social justice and the public good. But it also signals the importance of cultural politics as a pedagogical force for understanding how people buy into neoliberal ideology, how certain forms of agency are both suppressed and produced, how neoliberals work pedagogically to convince the public that consumer rights are more important than the rights people have as citizens and workers, and how pedagogy as a force for democratic change enables understanding, action and resistance.

> Let us suppose that a democracy, as complete, perfect, etc. as one
> might wish, might fall upon us from the heavens: this sort of democracy
> will not be able to endure for more than a few years if it does not
> engender individuals that correspond to it, ones that, first and foremost,
> are capable of making it function and reproducing it. There can be no
> democratic society without democratic *paideia*.[28]

Castoriadis was deeply concerned about what it meant to think about politics and
agency in light of the new conditions of capitalism that threatened to undermine
the promise of democracy at the end of the twentieth century. Moreover, he argues,
like Raymond Williams, that education in the broadest sense, is a principle feature
of politics because it provides the capacities, knowledge, skills and social relations
through which individuals recognize themselves as social and political agents. Linking
such a broad-based definition of education to issues of power and agency also raises
fundamental questions that go to the heart of any substantive notion of democracy:
how do issues of history, language, culture and identity work to articulate and
legitimate particular exclusions? If culture in this sense becomes the constituting
terrain for producing identities and constituting social subjects, education becomes
the strategic and positional mechanism through which such subjects are addressed,
positioned within social spaces, located within particular histories and experiences,
and always arbitrarily displaced and decentred as part of a pedagogical process that is
increasingly multiple, fractured and never homogenous.

Cornelius Castoriadis has over the last thirty years provided an enormous theoretical
service in analyzing the space of education as a constitutive site for democratic
struggle. Castoriadis pursues the primacy of education as a political force by focusing
on democracy as both the realized power of the people and as a mode of autonomy.
In the first instance, he insists that 'democracy means power of the people [...] a
regime aspiring to social and personal freedom'.[29] Democracy in this view suggests
more than a simply negative notion of freedom in which the individual is defended
against power. On the contrary, Castoriadis argues that any viable notion of
democracy must reject this passive attitude towards freedom with its view of power
as a necessary evil. In its place, he calls for a productive notion of power, one that is
central to embracing a notion of political agency and freedom that affirms the equal
opportunity of all to exercise political power in order to participate in shaping the
most important decisions affecting their lives.[30] He ardently rejected the increasing
'abandonment of the public sphere to specialists, to professional politicians'.[31] Just as
he rejected any conception of democracy that did not create the means for 'unlimited
interrogation in all domains' that closed off in 'advance not only every political
question as well as every philosophical one, but equally every ethical or aesthetic
question'.[32] Castoriadis refuses a notion of democracy restricted to the formalistic
processes of voting while at the same time arguing that the notion of participatory
democracy cannot remain narrowly confined to the political sphere.

Democracy, for Castoriadis, must also concern itself with the issue of cultural politics.
He rightly argues that progressives are required to address the ways in which every

society creates what he calls its 'social imaginary significations', which provide the structures of representations that offer individuals selected modes of identification, provide the standards for both the ends of action and the criteria for what is considered acceptable or unacceptable behaviour, while establishing the affective measures for mobilizing desire and human action.[33] The fate of democracy for Castoriadis was inextricably linked to the profound crisis of contemporary knowledge, characterized by its increasing commodification, fragmentation, privatization and the turn toward racial and patriotic conceits. As knowledge becomes abstracted from the demands of civic culture and is reduced to questions of style, ritual and image, it undermines the political, ethical and governing conditions for individuals and social groups to either participate in politics or construct those viable public spheres necessary for debate, collective action and solving urgent social problems. As Castoriadis suggests, the crisis of contemporary knowledge provides one of the central challenges to any viable notion of politics. He writes:

> Also in question is the relation of [...] knowledge to the society that produces it, nourishes it, is nourished by it, and risks dying of it, as well as the issues concerning for whom and for what this knowledge exists. Already at present these problems demand a radical transformation of society, and of the human being, at the same time that they contain its premises. If this monstrous tree of knowledge that modern humanity is cultivating more and more feverishly every day is not to collapse under its own weight and crush its gardener as it falls, the necessary transformations of man and society must go infinitely further than the wildest utopias have ever dared to imagine.[34]

Castoriadis was particularly concerned about how progressives might address the crisis of democracy in light of how social and political agents were being produced through dominant public pedagogies in a society driven by the glut of specialized knowledge, consumerism and a privatized notion of citizenship that no longer supported non-commercial values and increasingly dismissed as a constraint any view of society that emphasized public goods and social responsibility. What is crucial to acknowledge in Castoriadis's view of democracy is that the crisis of democracy cannot be separated from the dual crisis of representation and political agency. In a social order in which the production of knowledge, meaning and debate are highly restricted not only are the conditions for producing critical social agents limited, but also lost is the democratic imperative of affirming the primacy of ethics as a way of recognizing a social order's obligation to future generations. Ethics in this sense recognizes that the extension of power assumes a comparable extension in the field of ethical responsibility, a willingness to acknowledge that ethics means being able to answer in the present for actions that will be borne by generations in the future.[35]

Central to Castoriadis's work is the crucial acknowledgement that society creates itself through a multiplicity of organized pedagogical forms that provide the 'instituting social imaginary' or field of cultural and ideological representations through which social practices and institutional forms are endowed with meaning, generating certain ways of seeing the self and its possibilities in the world. Not only is the social individual constituted, in part, by internalizing such meanings, but he or she acts upon such meanings in order to also participate and, where possible, to change society. According to Castoriadis, politics within this framework becomes 'the collective activity whose object' is to put into question the explicit institutions of society while simultaneously creating the conditions for individual and social autonomy.[36] Castoriadis's unique contribution to democratic political theory lies in his keen understanding that autonomy is inextricably linked to forms of civic education which provide the conditions for bringing to light how explicit and implicit power can be used to open up or close down those public spaces that are essential for individuals to meet, address public interests, engage pressing social issues, and participate collectively in shaping public policy. In this view, civic education brings to light 'society's instituting power by rendering it explicit [...] it reabsorbs the political into politics as the lucid and deliberate activity whose object is the explicit [production] of society'.[37] According to Castoriadis, political agency involves learning how to deliberate, make judgements and exercise choices, particularly as the latter are brought to bear as critical activities that offer the possibility of change. Civic education as it is experienced and produced throughout a vast array of institutions provides individuals with the opportunity to see themselves as more than they simply are within the existing configurations of power of any given society. Every society has an obligation to provide citizens with the capacities, knowledge and skills necessary for them to be, as Aristotle claimed, 'capable of governing and being governed'.[38] A democracy cannot work if citizens are not autonomous, self-judging and independent, qualities that are indispensable for them to make vital judgements and choices about participating in and shaping decisions that effect everyday life, institutional reform and governmental policy. Hence, civic education becomes the cornerstone of democracy in that the very foundation of self-government is based on people not just having the 'typical right to participate; they should also be educated [in the fullest possible way] in order to be *able* to participate'.[39]

From a Pedagogy of Understanding to a Pedagogy of Intervention

It is not the knowledge of good and evil that we are missing; it is the skill and zeal to act on that knowledge which is conspicuously absent in this world of ours, in which dependencies, political responsibility and cultural values part ways and no longer hold each other in check.[40]

Williams and Castoriadis were clear that pedagogy and the active process of learning were central to any viable notion of citizenship and inclusive democracy. Pedagogy looms large for both of these theorists not as a technique or a priori set of methods but as a political and moral practice. As a political practice, pedagogy illuminates the relationship among power, knowledge and ideology, while self-consciously, if not self-critically, recognizing the role it plays as a deliberate attempt to influence how and what knowledge and identities are produced within particular sets of social relations. As a moral practice, pedagogy recognizes that what cultural workers, artists, activists, media workers and others teach cannot be abstracted from what it means to invest in public life, to presuppose some notion of the future, or to locate oneself in a public discourse.

The moral implications of pedagogy also suggest that our responsibility as public intellectuals cannot be separated from the consequences of the knowledge we produce, the social relations we legitimate, and the ideologies and identities we offer up to students. Refusing to decouple politics from pedagogy means, in part, that teaching in classrooms or in any other public sphere should not only simply honour the experiences students bring to such sites, including the classroom, but should also connect their experiences to specific problems that emanate from the material contexts of their everyday life. Pedagogy in this sense becomes performative in that it is not merely about deconstructing texts but about situating politics itself within a broader set of relations that addresses what it might mean to create modes of individual and social agency that enable rather than shut down democratic values, practices and social relations. Such a project recognizes not only the political nature of pedagogy, but also situates it within a call for intellectuals to assume responsibility for their actions, to link their teaching to those moral principles that allow us to do something about human suffering, as Susan Sontag has recently suggested.[41] Part of this task necessitates that cultural studies theorists and educators anchor their own work, however diverse, in a radical project that seriously engages the promise of an unrealized democracy against its really existing and radically incomplete forms. Of crucial importance to such a project is rejecting the assumption that theory can understand social problems without contesting their appearance in public life. Yet, any viable cultural politics needs a socially committed notion of injustice if we are to take seriously what it means to fight for the idea of the good society. I think Zygmunt Bauman is right in arguing that 'If there is no room for the idea of *wrong* society, there is hardly much chance for the idea of good society to be born, let alone make waves'.[42]

Cultural studies theorists need to be more forceful, if not committed, to linking their overall politics to modes of critique and collective action that address the presupposition that democratic societies are never too just or just enough, and such a recognition means that a society must constantly nurture the possibilities for self-critique, collective agency and forms of citizenship in which people play a fundamental role in critically discussing, administering and shaping the material relations of power and ideological forces that bear down on their everyday lives. At stake here is the task, as Jacques Derrida insists, of viewing the project of democracy as a promise, a possibility rooted in an ongoing struggle for economic, cultural and social justice.[43] Democracy in this instance is not a sutured or formalistic regime; it is the site of struggle itself. The struggle over creating an inclusive and just democracy can take many forms, offers no political guarantees, and provides an important normative dimension to politics as an ongoing process of democratization that never ends. Such a project is based on the realization that a democracy that is open to exchange, question and self-criticism never reaches the limits of justice. As Bauman observes:

> Democracy is not an institution, but essentially an anti-institutional force, a 'rupture' in the otherwise relentless trend of the powers-that-be to arrest change, to silence and to eliminate from the political process all those who have not been 'born 'into power [...] Democracy expresses itself in a continuous and relentless critique of institutions; democracy is an anarchic, disruptive element inside the political

system; essentially, a force for *dissent* and change. One can best recognize a democratic society by its constant complaints that it is *not* democratic enough.[44]

By linking education to the project of an unrealized democracy, cultural studies theorists who work in higher education can move beyond those approaches to pedagogy that reduce it to a methodology like 'teaching of the conflicts' or relatedly opening up a culture of questioning. In the most immediate sense, these positions fail to make clear the larger political, normative and ideological considerations that inform such views of education, teaching and visions of the future, assuming that education is predicated upon a particular view of the future that students should inhabit. Furthermore, both positions collapse the purpose and meaning of higher education, the role of educators as engaged scholars, and the possibility of pedagogy itself into a rather short-sighted and sometimes insular notion of method, particularly one that emphasizes argumentation and dialogue. There is a disquieting refusal in such discourses to raise broader questions about the social, economic and political forces shaping the very terrain of higher education – particularly unbridled market forces, or racist and sexist forces that unequally value diverse groups of students within relations of academic power, or what it might mean to engage pedagogy as a basis not merely for understanding but also for participating in the larger world. There is also a general misunderstanding of how teacher authority can be used to create the conditions for an education in democracy without necessarily falling into the trap of simply indoctrinating students.[45] For instance, liberal educator Gerald Graff believes that any notion of critical pedagogy that is self-conscious about its politics and engages students in ways that offer them the possibility for becoming critical – or what Lani Guinier calls the need to educate students 'to participate in civic life, and to encourage graduates to give back to the community, which through taxes, made their education possible'[46] – either leaves students out of the conversation or presupposes too much and simply represents a form of pedagogical tyranny. While Graff advocates strongly that educators create the educational practices that open up the possibility of questioning among students, he refuses to connect pedagogical conditions that challenge how they think at the moment to the next step of prompting them to think about changing the world around them so as to expand and deepen its democratic possibilities.

George Lipsitz criticizes academics such as Graff who believe that connecting academic work to social change is at best burden and, at worse, a collapse into a crude form of propagandizing suggesting that they are subconsciously educated to accept cynicism about the ability of ordinary people to change the conditions under which they live.[47] Teaching students how to argue, draw on their own experiences, or engage in rigorous dialogue says nothing about why they should engage in these actions in the first place. How the culture of argumentation and questioning relates to giving students the tools they need to fight oppressive forms of power, make the world a more meaningful and just place, and develop a sense of social responsibility is missing in work like Graff's because this is part of the discourse of political education, which Graff simply equates to indoctrination or speaking to the converted.[48] Here propaganda and critical pedagogy collapse into each other. Propaganda is generally used to misrepresent knowledge, promote biased knowledge, or produce a view of politics that appears beyond question and critical engagement. While no pedagogical intervention should fall to the level of propaganda, a pedagogy which attempts to empower critical citizens can't and shouldn't avoid politics. Pedagogy must address the relationship between politics and agency, knowledge and power, subject positions and values, and learning and social change while always being open to debate, resistance and a culture of questioning. Liberal educators committed to simply raising questions have no language for linking learning to forms of public scholarship that would enable students to consider the important relationship between democratic public life and education, politics and learning. Disabled by a depoliticizing, if not slavish allegiance to a teaching methodology, they have little idea of how to encourage students pedagogically to enter the sphere of the political, enabling them to think about how they might participate in a democracy by taking what they learn 'into new locations – a third grade classroom, a public library, a legislator's office, a park'[49] or for that matter taking on collaborative projects that address the myriad of problems citizens face in a diminishing democracy. In spite of the professional pretence to neutrality, academics need to do more pedagogically than simply teach students how to be adept at forms of argumentation. Students need to argue and question, but they need much more from their educational experience. The pedagogy of argumentation in and of itself guarantees nothing but it is an essential step towards opening up the space of resistance towards authority, teaching students to think critically about the world around them, and recognizing interpretation and dialogue as a condition for social intervention and transformation in the service of an unrealized democratic order. As Amy Gutmann brilliantly argues, education is always political because it is connected to the acquisition of agency, the ability to struggle with ongoing relations of power, and is a precondition for creating informed and critical citizens. For Gutmann, educators need to link education to democracy and recognize pedagogy as an ethical and political practice tied to modes of authority in which the 'democratic state recognizes the value of political education in predisposing [students] to accept those ways of life that are consistent with sharing the rights and responsibilities of citizenship in a democratic society'.[50] This is not a notion of education tied to the alleged neutrality of teaching methods but to a vision of pedagogy that is directive and interventionist on the side of reproducing a democratic society. Democratic societies need educated citizens who are steeped in more than the skills of argumentation. And it is precisely this democratic project that affirms the critical function of education and refuses to narrow its goals and aspirations to methodological considerations. This is what makes critical pedagogy different from training. And it is precisely the failure to connect learning to its democratic functions and goals that provides rationales for pedagogical approaches that strip the meaning of what it means to be educated from its critical and democratic possibilities.

Raymond Williams and Castoriadis recognized that the crisis of democracy was not only about the crisis of culture but also the crisis of pedagogy and education. Cultural studies theorists would do well to take account of the profound transformations taking place in the public sphere and reclaim pedagogy as a central category of cultural politics. The time has come for cultural studies theorists to distinguish professional caution from political cowardice and recognize that their obligations extend beyond deconstructing texts or promoting a culture of questioning. These are important pedagogical interventions, but they do not go far enough. We need to link knowing with action, learning with social engagement, and this requires addressing the responsibilities that come with teaching students and others to fight for an inclusive and radical democracy by recognizing that education in the broadest sense is not just about understanding, however critical, but also provides the conditions for assuming the responsibilities we have as citizens to expose human misery and to eliminate the conditions that produce it. I think Bauman is quite right in suggesting that as engaged cultural workers, we need to take up our work as part of a broader democratic project in which the good society:

> is a society which thinks it is not just enough, which questions the sufficiency of any achieved level of justice and considers justice always to be a step or more ahead. Above all, it is a society which reacts angrily to any case of injustice and promptly sets about correcting it.[51]

Matters of responsibility, social action, and political intervention do not simply develop out of social critique but also forms of self-critique. The relationship between knowledge and power, on the one hand, and scholarship and politics, on the other, should always be self-reflexive about its effects, how it relates to the larger world, whether or not it is open to new understandings, and what it might mean pedagogically to take seriously matters of individual and social responsibility. In short, this project points to the need for educators to articulate cultural studies as not only a resource for theoretical competency and critical understanding, but also as a pedagogical practice that addresses the possibility of interpretation as intervention in the world.

Neoliberalism not only places capital and market relations in a no-mans land beyond the reach of compassion, ethics and decency, it also undermines those basic elements of the social contract and the political and pedagogical relations it presupposes in which self-reliance, confidence in others, and a trust in the longevity of democratic institutions provide the basis for modes of individual autonomy, social agency and critical citizenship. One of the most serious challenges faced by cultural studies is the need to develop a new language and theoretical tools for contesting a variety of forms of domination put into play by neoliberalism in the new millennium. Part of this challenge demands recognizing that the struggles over cultural politics cannot be divorced from the contestations and struggles put into play through the forces of dominant economic and cultural institutions and their respective modes of education. Cultural studies advocates must address the challenge of how to problematize and pluralize the political, engage new sites of pedagogy as crucial, strategic public spheres, and situate cultural studies within an ongoing project that recognizes that the crisis of democracy is about the interrelated crises of politics, culture and education.

Notes

[1] Zygmunt Bauman, *Work, Consumerism and the New Poor* (Philadelphia: Open University press, 1998), pp.97–98.

[2] James Rule, 'Markets, in Their Place', *Dissent* (Winter, 1998), p.31.

[3] Zygmunt Bauman, *The Individualized Society* (London: Polity Press, 2001), p.107.

[4] Bauman, *The Individualized Society*.

[5] Pierre Bourdieu, *Language and Symbolic Power* (Cambridge, MA: Harvard University Press, 2001), p.127.

[6] Pierre Bourdieu, *Language and Symbolic Power*, p.128.

[7] For some general theoretical principles for addressing the new sites of pedagogy, see Jeffrey

R. DiLeo, Walter Jacobs and Amy Lee, 'The Sites of Pedagogy', *Symploke* 10:1–2 (2003), pp.7–12.

[8] William Greider, 'The Right's Grand Ambition: Rolling Back the 20th Century', *The Nation* (May 12, 2003), p.11.

[9] One interesting analysis on the contingent nature of democracy and public space can be found in Rosalyn Deutsche, *Evictions: Art and Spatial Politics* (Cambridge, MA: The MIT Press, 1998).

[10] Cited in Robert Dreyfuss, 'Grover Norquist: "Field Marshal" of the Bush Plan', *The Nation* (May 14, 2001), p.1. Available on line: http://www.thenation.com/doc.mhtml?i=20010514&s=dreyfuss

[11] Raymond Williams, *Communications*, revised edition (New York: Barnes & Noble, 1966), p.15.

[12] Benjamin R Barber, 'A Failure of Democracy, Not Capitalism', *The New York Times* (Monday, July 29, 2002), p.A23.

[13] Bob Herbert, 'The Art of False Impression', *The New York Times* (August 11, 2003), p.A17.

[14] W.E.B. Du Bois, *Against Racism: Unpublished Essays, Papers, Addresses, 1887–1961*, Herbert Aptheker [ed] (Amherst: University of Massachusetts Press, 1985).

[15] Cornelius Castoriadis cited in Zygmunt Bauman, *The Individualized Society*, p.127.

[16] Michele Barrett, *Imagination in Theory* (New York: New York University Press, 1999), p.161.

[17] Zygmunt Bauman and Keith Tester, *Conversations with Zygmunt Bauman* (Malden: Polity Press, 2001), p.32.

[18] On the importance of problematizing and pluralizing the political, see Jodi Dean, 'The Interface of Political Theory and Cultural Studies', in Jodi Dean [ed], *Cultural Studies and Political Theory* (Ithaca: Cornell University Press, 2000), pp.1–19.

[19] Robert W. McChesney and John Nichols, *Our Media not Theirs: The Democratic struggle Against Corporate Media* (New York: Seven Stories Press, 2002).

[20] Zygmunt Bauman, *In Search of Politics* (Stanford, CA: Stanford University Press, 1999).

[21] Nick Couldry, 'In the Place of a Common Culture, What', *Review of Education/Pedagogy/Cultural Studies* (in press), p.6.

[22] Raymond Williams, 'Preface to Second Edition', *Communications* (New York: Barnes and Noble, 1967), pp.15–16.

[23] Williams, 'Preface to Second Edition', p.14.

[24] See especially, Raymond Williams, *Marxism and Literature* (New York: Oxford University Press, 1977); Raymond Williams, *The Year 2000* (New York: Pantheon, 1983).

[25] Williams, *Marxism and Literature*.

[26] See Tony Bennett, *Culture: A Reformer's Science* (Thousand Oaks: Sage, 1998), p.223.

[27] Antonio Gramsci, *Selections from the Prison Notebooks* (New York International Press, 1971), p.350.

[28] Cornelius Castoriadis, 'Democracy as Procedure and Democracy as Regime', *Constellations* 4:1 (1997), p.10.

[29] Cornelius Castoriadis, 'The Problem of Democracy Today', *Democracy and Nature* Vol. 8 (April 1996), p.19.

[30] Cornelius Castoriadis, 'The Nature and Value of Equity', *Philosophy, Politics, Autonomy: Essays in Political Philosophy* (New York: Oxford University Press, 1991), pp.124–142.

[31] Cornelius Castoriadis, *The World in Fragments*, trans. David Ames Curtis [ed] (Stanford: Stanford University Press, 1997), p.91.

[32] Both quotations are taken from Cornelius Castoriadis, 'Culture in a Democratic Society', in David Ames Curtis [ed], *The Castoriadis Reader* (Malden, MA: Blackwell, 1997), pp.343, 341.

[33] Cornelius Castoriadis, 'The Crisis of the Identification Process', *Thesis Eleven* 49 (May 1997), pp.87–88.

[34] Cornelius Castoriadis, 'The Anticipated Revolution', in David Ames Curtis [ed], *Political and Social Writings, Vol. 3*, trans. David Ames Curtis (Minneapolis: University of Minnesota Press, 1993), pp.153–154.

[35] John Binde, 'Toward an Ethic of the Future', *Public Culture* 12:1 (2000), p.65.

[36] Cornelius Castoriadis, 'The Greek Polis and the Creation of Democracy', *Philosophy, Politics, Autonomy*, p.102.

[37] Castoriadis, 'The Greek Polis and the Creation of Democracy'; 'Power, Politics, and Autonomy', *Philosophy, Politics, Autonomy*, pp.144–145.

[38] Castoriadis, 'Power, Politics, and Autonomy'; 'Democracy as Procedure and Democracy as Regime', p.15. It is crucial here to note that Castoriadis develops both his notion of democracy and the primacy of education in political life directly from his study of ancient Greek democracy.

[39] Castoriadis, 'Power, Politics, and Autonomy'; 'The Problem of Democracy Today', p.24.

[40] Bauman and Tester, *Conversations with Zygmunt Bauman*, p.131.

[41] Susan Sontag, 'Courage and Resistance', *The Nation* (May 5, 2003), pp.11–14.

[42] Zygmunt Bauman, *Society under Siege* (Malden, MA: Blackwell: 2002), p.170.

[43] Jacques Derrida, 'Intellectual Courage: An Interview', trans. Peter Krapp, *Culture Machine*, Volume 2 (2000), pp.1–15.

[44] Bauman, *The Individualized Society*, pp.54–55.

[45] Gerald Graff appears to have made a career out of this issue by either misrepresenting the work of Paulo Freire and others, citing theoretical work by critical educators that is outdated and could be corrected by reading anything they might have written in the last five years, creating caricatures of

their work, or by holding up as an example of what people in critical pedagogy do (or more generally anyone who links pedagogy and politics) the most extreme and ludicrous examples. For more recent representations of this position, see Gerald Graff, 'Teaching Politically Without Political Correctness', *Radical Teacher* 58 (Fall, 2000), pp.26–30; Gerald Graff, *Clueless in Academe* (New Haven: Yale University Press, 2003).

[46] Lani Guinier, 'Democracy Tested', *The Nation* (May 5, 2003) p.6. Guinier's position is in direct opposition to that of Graff and is acolytes. For instance, see 'A Conversation Between Lani Guinier and Anna Deavere Smith, Rethinking Power, Rethinking Theater', *Theater* 31:3 (Winter, 2002), pp.31–45.

[47] George Lipsitz, 'Academic Politics and Social Change', in Jodi Dean [ed], *Cultural Studies and Political Theory* (Ithaca: Cornell University Press, 2000), pp.81–82.

[48] For a more detailed response to this kind of watered down pedagogical practice, see Stanley Aronowitz, *The Knowledge Factory* (Boston: Beacon Press, 2000); Henry A. Giroux, *The Abandoned Generation: Democracy Beyond the Culture of Fear* (New York: Palgrave, 2003).

[49] An Interview with Julie Ellison, 'New Public Scholarship in the Arts and Humanities', *Higher Education Exchange* (2002), p.20.

[50] Amy Gutmann, *Democratic Education* (Princeton: Princeton University Press, 1998), p.42.

[51] Bauman and Tester, *Conversations with Zygmunt Bauman*, p.63.

Henry A. Giroux is the Global TV Network Chaired Professor in Communication at McMaster University in Canada. His most recent books include: *Breaking Into the Movies: Film and the Culture of Politics* (Basil Blackwell, 2002), *Public Spaces/Private Lives: Democracy Beyond 9/11* (Rowman and Littlefield, 2002) and *The Abandoned Generation: Democracy Beyond the Culture of Fear* (Palgrave, 2003). His primary research areas are: cultural studies, youth studies, critical pedagogy, popular culture, social theory and the politics of higher education.

parallax, 2004, vol. 10, no. 2, 90–99

Precarious Intellectuals: On the re-structuring of academic life and the *précarisation* of the 'free researchers' in Austria

Roman Horak

Towards a new 'world class university'

As the new statutes[1] that were to lay down the structure of the University of Vienna were withdrawn shortly before Christmas 2003 and a – temporary – extension of the validity of the old regulations agreed upon, the rather abstruse mixture of neo-liberal impetus, incompetent planning and conservative strategy that has characterized the right-wing conservative Austrian government again and again since its accession to power in February 2000,[2] once more became apparent. This is not the place to present a list of the various similar initiatives of this government. It will suffice to note that in their totality they represent a profound upheaval in Austria's political culture and the political system and that this was entirely intentional, as all the persistent talk of a 'turning point' bears out.

This short text intends to outline the changes to the situation of intellectuals and academic life in Austria, especially for the special 'species' of 'free researchers'.[3] While their situation and career perspectives have never been all that rosy, these have deteriorated drastically in the last few years. This has to do with the academic policy of the government in general, but more particularly with its university policy, as many 'free researchers' receive as external lecturers a minimal basic income that now threatens to dry up completely because universities no longer have the financial resources to even employ external lecturers. I will attempt to outline and comment on this new legislation as a form of introduction into my topic.

The new structure mentioned above that is to be imposed on the universities[4] represents a further step in the implementation of the University Bill (UG 02) that was passed on 11 July, 2002 with the votes from the People's Party (*ÖVP*) and the Freedom Party (*FPÖ*) and became law on 1 October, 2002. It prescribes that the Austrian universities should no longer be directly dependent on the federal administration and transformed into a legal entity under civil law (the keywords being 'autonomy' and 'full legal status'). The universities are to receive three-year global budgets with a performance related component; they will draw up performance agreements with the Federal Ministry for Education, Science and Culture and shall become employers in their own right. In future the universities are to be administered by a newly created university council, a rector and a senate. While the direct authority of the senate will

parallax
ISSN 1353-4645 print/ISSN 1460-700X online © 2004 Taylor & Francis Ltd
http://www.tandf.co.uk/journals
DOI: 10.1080/1353464042000208549

be limited, the university council and the rector will be the true centres of power in the new university. The former will function as the highest controlling body in every university, which will elect the rector and approve development plans for the university. The university councils will consist of five members, three of which will be from the university itself and two from the relevant ministry. According to the law, the members of the university council should be persons 'who because of their outstanding knowledge and experience can contribute towards the implementation of the objectives and assignment of the university'.[5] Politicians and anyone belonging to the universities concerned cannot be members. The appointment of a number of persons of reactionary opinions in the past year not only caused some excitement in the media but also demonstrated above all the intention of the government[6] to install conservatives in key positions.

In comparison to the legislation up to now, the University Bill of 2002 significantly enhances the position of the rector, with the whole operative business lying in future in his hands and those of his deputies, similar to the function of the directors of private enterprises.

This choice of structure is by no means coincidental, nor can the continually repeated talk of reform,[7] full legal status and autonomy, or even 'a world class university',[8] disguise that the underlying intention went in another direction. No one has put this in a nutshell as effectively as Claus Raidl, an executive of the *Böhler-Uddeholm* concern and more recently a member of the technical college council, when he formulated the objective of the above reform as follows:

'We have to finally plant market economic ideas into people's heads'.[9]

This is undoubtedly a point of view that illustrates a European trend. Everywhere universities have long been in the throes of change that also threatens the existence of the social and cultural sciences.[10] In Austria, too, plans to privatize the universities and transform them into entrepreneurial institutions have existed for over a decade. Already under the Social-Democratic coalition the Christian-Conservative science minister presented the first plans for a 'reform of the universities' at the beginning of the 1990s. At the time a large part of the 'reform' package had to be withdrawn because of the concerted opposition of all the representative bodies of the universities. So, too, the proposal of full legal status that was made in 1999 met with little support both inside and outside the universities. When, however, a paper with similar content was presented to the rector's conference and the Federal Ministry for Education, Science and Culture at the beginning of 2000 the situation had changed. Parts of the universities (especially the rectors of the larger universities) took up the approach that had been promoted by the ministry for ten years and documented a change of hegemony. The discourse on 'market forces' that had come to dominate now became the predominant model for public debate.

Politically this boils down to a retraction of the democratic advances introduced by the university reform of 1975, which – incorporating the sense of change of the 1970s[11] – included codetermination for the students and the so-called middle level (assistants and lecturers) in diverse aspects of tertiary education (curricula, professorships and the appointment of professors) and thus a reduction of the power of full professors. The new law has now dissolved the relevant institutions and codetermination has *de facto* been abolished. A wholesale feeling of fatigue and despondency – especially among the students – seems to have spread throughout the universities. Of course, voices were raised against the reform,[12] but the neo-conservative brew consisting of efficiency talk, the call for 'new public management' (the new mantra), and networks of learning, together with rather stale rhetoric concerning the cultural assignment of universities[13] had probably won the upper hand.

Critical Research outside the Universities and the Beginning of Cultural Studies in Vienna

One of the peculiarities of the Austrian academic world is the increasing numbers of young researchers in the social and cultural sciences that have been working on a freelance basis since the late seventies/early eighties without being employed by the universities. The reasons for this development are manifold and, paradoxically, are linked to the reform of the universities in the 'Social-Democratic decade' of the seventies. The opening of the universities and the so-called explosion in tertiary education during those years brought with them a marked increase in university staff, but only a minor increase in critical and innovative potential.[14] This, in my opinion, was due largely to two factors. Firstly, there was the harassment and expulsion of numerous scientists during the period of National Socialism. The already secure dominance of conservative (and usually mediocre) university teachers continued after the end of WWII. That part of the Austrian Jewish intelligentsia which managed to survive the Holocaust was not encouraged to return; many who had been forced to leave the country were understandably reluctant to go back to Austria. Secondly, the professors were dominated by Christian-Conservatives who largely retained control even during the reform years. The critical young intelligentsia that was able to assume important professorial posts in West Germany in the wage of the student revolution of the late sixties, was too small in number and too weak[15] in Austria to have a similar influence on the universities here. The recruitment of new staff continued to follow almost feudal principles.

> Assistant posts were traditionally filled according to the method of awarding a fiefdom. The lords that decided here on [a candidate's] career prospects and life, had every motive not to recruit newcomers that might put them in the shade. Thus, there was always a bias towards craven mediocrity.[16]

For this reason it is not surprising that the 'dissatisfaction with the universities both in terms of their ability to solve problems and their political affiliation in the seventies led to an increased emphasis on non-university research', as Lukas Mitterauer writes. He also adds that large institutes[17] were supported, which from today's point of view only differed from the universities in that they offered no academic tuition.[18]

This is perhaps a little imprecise as a number of these facilities now offer post-graduate education, but this reveals what happened in the eighties. Many of the post-1968 generation of students finished their studies at the beginning of this decade. Those among them for whom neither the universities nor the more practice-oriented large institutions outside the universities offered suitable career perspectives began to look for their niches[19] as individual researchers or in small groups, where they could work without direct control of their content and methods. Research funds were also available – albeit to a rather restricted extent – in these years. Optimism and the will to try out something new were pervasive.

The history of the Institute for Cultural Studies (IKUS) in Vienna, probably the first of its kind in the German-speaking world, should be seen against this background, which I shall now relate in my capacity of contemporary participant.

The IKUS grew from a friendship between its three founders (Wolfgang Reiter, Kurt Stocker and the author), who shared rooms together for a time. They were also conscious that the conventional academic career ladder was not for them. So they gave their breakfast talk of football a practical application by applying for and receiving research funds for a study of 'soccer hooliganism' and began their cooperation in social science in 1983. Their preoccupation with football violence led them to read English texts emanating from the Centre for Contemporary Cultural Studies (CCCS) in Birmingham. They studied the essays on youth culture and diverse working papers with a considerable time lag but did not leave it at that. Above all they read Raymond Williams and Stuart Hall in English, particularly the latter's work on 'Thatcherism' and, a little later, his contributions to the debate on the 'New Times', which appeared in 'Marxism Today' and the 'New Statesman'.

The concomitant and – selective – delayed appropriation of cultural studies and the growing conviction that further presence within the scientific community and resulting financial support of diverse official sponsors could only be ensured with the aid of a formal structure led to the foundation of the 'Institute for Cultural Studies' in August 1985. As an independent non-university research facility it was organized in the form of an association and had an advisory board consisting of well-known Austrian and German social scientists which symbolically tied it to the academic world. The institute grew; office space was rented; the thematic spectrum broadened[20]; and the number of associates who worked to different extents on the individual projects increased.

A study of 'multi-culturalism'[21] was produced and published by IKUS in 1993, but more important than this book project was a series that had been planned as a scientific bi-annual journal in the late eighties that would make the special features of IKUS public. The IKUS-Lectures began to appear from autumn 1992 onwards and documented in 22 editions the debates organized by the institute. The titles range from the 'aesthetics of marginalization' to 'radio culture', from 'global migration' to 'right-wing extremism and education', which reflect one of the programmatic principles that gave rise to IKUS – namely, thematic scope.

The resulting public echo – even glossy zeitgeist magazines published photographs of the ambitious young cultural scientists and their institute – and the wide range of activities could not banish the growing difficulties that the institute had to combat, particularly at the beginning of the nineties. They ranged from internal conflicts (which could be interpreted as power struggles over the future direction of IKUS) to the financial problems that had accompanied us from the beginning (apart from a secretary, none of the IKUS contributors was employed by the institute; the researchers had to pay private income tax on their income and were neither eligible for health insurance nor retirement benefits), together with the often trying conflicts with the representatives of potential sponsors, not least those of the scientific bureaucracy.

When the end was approaching a series of seminars entitled 'Contemporary Cultural Studies' was launched in autumn 1993 following the model of the IKUS-Lectures. As was the case in the 'Lectures', the intention was to publish all the lectures, but this was not to be: of the seven lectures and discussions planned only the first three actually took place. The participants were H. Gustav Klaus, Rolf Lindner, Nora Räthzel (on cultural studies in German-speaking areas), Ros Gill, David Morley (on ethnography/ discourse analysis) and Les Back, Phil Cohen (on racism/ethnicity). The planned seminars on popular culture, sexuality, gender, feminism, politics and cultural institutions had to be cancelled for lack of funds. Finally, in September 1994 Lawrence Grossberg who had been chosen as one of the tutors for the workshop on the 'history and theory of cultural studies' held the closing lecture. Grossberg's presentation was published in German translation together with the texts of Lindner, Klaus and Räthzel in the 17th and 19th editions of the IKUS-Lectures as the swan song of institute. With the end of the year 1994 came the closure of the institute.

The necessity of closure was sealed by the decision of the conservative science minister at the time, who rode his ideological hobbyhorse – the culture and politics of central Europe (a covert articulation of hegemonic Austrian aspirations concerning the neighbouring countries of the former East Block) – by founding the *Interdisziplinäres Forschungszentrum Kulturwissenschaften*/International Research Center for Cultural Studies[22] (IFK) in 1993 and at the same time starving the IKUS of funds. The whole situation had changed: the number of freelance social and human scientists had risen drastically, without the necessary funding for free research increasing proportionately. More and more colleagues tried to earn some form of basic income and get access to a permanent university post by accepting short-term lecturing jobs at university faculties.

> Thus by the mid-1990s a competitive academic market for educational products was firmly in place, created by the Austrian government (which effectively exercised control over the university system) through the underfunding/understaffing of the universities and the concomitant build-up of a parallel structure of funding research for external lecturers with a tenuous relationship to the universities. In 1994/95, external lecturers taught more than half of humanities courses at the University of Vienna, but their contract situation continued to be characterized by the ambivalent and hazardous conditions of private, part-time employment (often dependent on personal relationships, the scarcity and perceived desirability of the product/course offered and such unfathomable features as personal reputation and the quality of academic work as well as the complete absence of transparent, or indeed any, structures of research or teaching evaluations).[23]

Two organizations were called into being by freelance researchers to protect the interests of those involved. The first, which had a more social sciences orientation, was the '*Forum Sozialforschung*'[24] (Forum for Social Science) which was founded in 1992 with the help of IKUS. In the meantime it seems to have terminated its activities – its homepage is no longer online. The second initiative, the *Interessengemeinschaft externer LektorInnen und freier WissenschafterInnen* (the Association of External Lectors and Free Academics), which was largely a representative of researchers and external lecturers in the humanities, was set up in 1996 and still exists.[25]

Precarious Intellectuals

With the inauguration of the right-wing conservative government in February 2000 the position of free researchers once again deteriorated dramatically. It became even more difficult to obtain lecturing posts – the university 'reform' was outlined earlier – and funds available for autonomous social and humanities research (which are after all mainly controlled by the state) began to dry up. While numerous free researchers could gain some basic income between 1998 and the beginning of 2003 in the research initiative in cultural sciences of the Science Ministry (there was a total of over fifty projects with around 150 academics participating),[26] there is now hardly any prospect of all those who have been working for these projects, many of them for years, staying in the academic world. This does not merely represent a pretty obvious destruction of human capital, to use a contemporary coinage, but above all an extremely cynical attitude towards young people – a large proportion of those affected are in their thirties and at the start of their academic careers which will now have to end abruptly.

Let us turn to a foreign voice at this juncture to avoid the possible accusation of this being just another example of the typically Austrian penchant for over-dramatization. A report initiated in July 2000 by the Austrian Ministry of Science and organized by the European Science Foundation (ESF) and an international commission on the evaluation of Austrian contemporary history research (between 1990 and 2000) stated the following in its concluding remarks:

> There is [...] a growing subculture of independent, mostly young historians, who, although they certainly produce a considerable share of innovative and research achievements, have no prospect of establishing themselves in institutionally regulated university work. While they are contracted time and again on a subsidiary basis, they have no hope of being integrated into institutionalized research. In terms of scientific and social policy, this lack of perspective is exceptional and disturbing. This group presents itself in public with a mixture of sentimentality and aggression (e.g. at the hearing in Vienna). This is also a sign of a social problem in the scientific community.[27]

What is described here in the dry language of an evaluation report does not just apply to contemporary history, it affects pretty much all areas of the social sciences and humanities – and it affects above all a growing number of people whom one can count amongst the 'precarious intellectuals'. Anne and Marine Rambach relate an account of this phenomenon in their book of the same name,[28] which caused serious debate in France among the members of a generation who were not being offered what had once been stable careers but had to struggle with seeming independence after their university studies. This includes above all the representatives of the 25 to 35 year-old age group who are active in journalism, cultural activities, film and television, independent research and the so-called 'creative industries'. Their lives are characterized by a chasm between their high social status and their miserable material situation. On the other hand, the two authors argue, the fact that in this case economic setbacks are not accompanied by social marginalization makes it difficult for this group to organize itself politically.

What is symptomatic about the situation of the precarious intellectuals is the very fact that the members of this social group produce 'cultural goods' without getting the symbolic revenue from those who make use of what they produce. Very often their names are not even mentioned on the published (and official) versions of the reports they wrote or in the TV-documentaries they provided the essential research for.

Particularly striking, however, are the lives of those we have called 'free researchers' in this contribution. Since they are – via research grants – directly or indirectly dependent on state institutions (Universities, research funds etc.) they do not have many alternatives if they want to stay in academia (i. e. work on what they think is interesting, important and intellectually challenging). There is not – and never was – such a thing as a 'market' (in 'free market' societies) for the goods they produce, but, nevertheless, their situation has become worse.

It would be too simple to blame it all on the new Austrian government. What has changed – long before February 2000 – is the dominant understanding of the state. With a certain delay the neo-liberal concept of the nation-state reached Austria in the 1980s; the rhetoric of de-regulation etc. did not start with the conservative government, it only became louder and more obvious when it came to power. Its politics had already been quite effective during the coalition of the social-democratic party SPÖ with the Christian conservatives ÖVP in the late 1980s. New, however, are both the pace with which these politics are being implemented, and the conservative drive to rescind the achievements of the 'social-democratic era' of the 1970s. This, of course, refers not only to the educational system; it includes literally every political field from media politics to issues of social security. Maybe it does make sense to use the term 'Austro-Thatcherism' as Austria's leading political scientist Anton Pelinka[29] and Chantal Mouffe[30] (both coming from different theoretical backgrounds) have in order to analyze this situation as a particular variant of neo-liberal politics. But whatever notion we use, it must not be forgotten, firstly, that it is one moment of the Western capitalist post-89 project, and, secondly, that these developments can only be countered effectively by elaborating new strategies and new forms of co-operation. As one representative of the Austrian 'free researchers' has put it with reference to the particular situation of the precarious intellectuals:

> Political strategies can only hope for success when they form in
> new alliances to fight for the creation or return of elementary social
> rights. Many rights, which from the point of view of those precarious

individuals on the inside are seen as their rights, are threatened by loss. Whether it be the safeguarding of tolerable working conditions or codetermination in businesses, or the defense or reinforcement of unemployment insurance or the introduction of a basic wage: these objectives can only become politically feasible through the alliance between seemingly privileged internals and the precarious individuals on the periphery. Nothing could be more detrimental to the realization of political goals than conflicts between those 'inside' and those 'outside', the 'father generation' and the 'heirs to 68'.[31]

Notes

[1] Instead of the present seven faculties (without medicine) plus four interfaculty-institutes the University of Vienna will have 18 faculties without any prescribed institute allocation. In other words, many institutes will be abolished. Instead of the present three levels (rector, faculties, institutes), a 'flat hierarchy' with two levels consisting of the rector and the faculties will be introduced, which de facto means a change in the balance of power to the advantage of the upper level of the hierarchy.

[2] The national election of 24 November, 2002 meant a considerable loss of votes for the populist Freedom Party, but the conservative majority remained in place and the coalition under the Christian-Conservative chancellor Wolfgang Schuessel formed the new cabinet.

[3] The author of these lines belonged to this group for 18 years and has only been permanently employed at the university since March, 2001. Thus, he knows both sides and is willing to admit that his personal situation, in spite of circumstances that are less than favourable for the universities, has improved.

[4] As a result of the transformation of the medical faculties at the universities of Vienna, Graz and Innsbruck into independent universities, the number of universities in Austria has increased from 18 to 21.

[5] § 19, Abs. 4.

[6] The quickest and deepest possible positioning of conservative elites in key positions in the state and society seems to be one of the main activities of the present government. This no doubt also characterizes other political parties, but the shamelessness with which it is carried out at present is entirely new.

[7] The distortion of the term 'reform' from meaning an increased wellbeing for the majority, to the present opposite connotation could form the subject of a study paper.

[8] The appellation 'world class university' was produced by the government, which saw this as an articulation of its own intentions for its university policy. Poorly heated auditoria, falling budgets for publications, exhibitions, etc. at the university where I lecture produce a totally different picture. For all those who enjoy shoddy entertainment: www.weltklasse-uni.at but they have to at least have a grasp of basic German. An English version has not yet been attempted – *vide* 'world class'!

[9] Quoted from the website of the Independent Student Representatives for All Austria: http://oeh.ac.at/oeh/oeh (as of 12 December, 2003). The president of the federation of industrialists, the chairman of Cybertron Telekom AG and the general secretary of the federation of industrialists have all made similar remarks (cf. IV Newsroom, program of 13 December, 2001, www.iv-net.at/static/info/service/zkuni_pdi.pdf [as of 15 December, 2003]) and the working group 'engagierte Unternehmer' in a letter of 30 November, 2001 to the relevant ministerial staff (www.weltklasse-uni.at/upload/attachments/228.pdf [as of 10 November, 2003]).

[10] The new priorities are revealed in the budget allocations for the year 2004: while the University of Economics has received a 16% increase over the previous year, the University of Applied Arts has to plan for a reduction of 8–10% in real terms.

[11] The rector of the University of Vienna has – on the side, but hardly accidentally – made the remark that the point now was to free the institutes of the 'spirit of 75'. Cf. Thomas König, 'Flache Diskurse – Neu Flache Diskurse – neue Organisationseinheiten', *Malmö* 17 (November, 2003), p. 6. The government, which had abolished study fees in the seventies on socio-political grounds to allow everyone access to the universities, reintroduced them in 2001. Enrolment at a university in Austria is no longer free of charge since the winter term of 2001/02.

[12] Cf. Ada Pellert, 'Stell Dir vor, es gibt Hochschulmanagement und keiner will es' (www.weltklasse-uni.at/upload/attachments/243.pdf [as of 27 November, 2003]), or Max Preglau, 'Die Universitätsreform – schädlich für Wissenschaft

und Gesellschaft', (www2.uibk.ac.at/service/c115/aktuelles/unireform/ [as of 15 November, 2003]).

[13] Cf. Erich Hödl, 'Universitätsreform 2002', in H. Hösele, H. Lopatka and R.Schnider [eds], *Steirisches Jahrbuch für Politik 2002* (Graz, 2003) (here quoted from: www.bdr.tugraz.at/hoedl/Artikel/univreform.htm [as of 20 December, 2003]).

[14] Cf. L. Mitterauer, 'Positionierung des Forums Sozialforschung', *Forums Sozialforschung (Hg.), Positionierung der außeruniversitären Sozialforschung* (Wien, 1999), p.17ff.

[15] Unlike most other Western European countries '1968' is associated more in Austria with artistic than political revolution.

[16] H. G. Zilian, 'Zwei Welten: universitäre und außeruniversitäre Wissenschaft', (www.univie.ac.at/OEGS-Kongress-2000/on-line-Publiaktion/Zilian.pdf [as of 15 November, 2003]).

[17] Let me mention two of them briefly. The *Institut für Höhere Studien* (IHS)/Institute for Advanced Studies (cf. www.ihs.ac.at [as of 10 December, 2003]) was set up in 1963 after some preliminary setbacks. There was resistance on the part of the university (above all the Faculty for Law) and the Christian-Conservative People's Party (*ÖVP*), who feared a 'Socialist enclave' in the conservative university system and no doubt because of anti-Semitic and anti-American prejudice. The problem was solved by filling all important positions with representatives of the two major parties, the Social-Democratic Socialist Party (*SPÖ*) and the conservative *ÖVP*. Lazarsfeld's initial plan to introduce disciplines such as Social Psychology, Empirical Political Research and Industrial Relations that were not taught at the university was dropped and the dominance of economic sciences has remained to the present. Cf. Christian Fleck, 'Wie Neues nicht entsteht. Die Gründung des Instituts für Höhere Studien durch Exil-Österreicher und die Ford-Foundation', *Österreichische Zeitschrift für Geschichtswissenschaft* 11:Heft 1 (2000), pp.129–178; Helmut Kramer, 'Wie Neues doch entstanden ist. Zur Gründung und zu den ersten Jahren des Instituts für Höhere Studien', *Österreichische Zeitschrift für Geschichtswissenschaft* 13:Heft 3 (2002), pp.110–132. The second institute is the 'European Centre for Social Welfare Policy and Research', which was set up in 1974 as a result of an agreement between the UN and the Austrian Federal Government (cf. www.euro.centre.org [as of 12 December, 2003]).

[18] Mitterauer, 'Positionierungen', p.18.

[19] Cf. M. Marschik, 'Über das Leben und Forschen in Nischen', *Forums Sozialforschung (Hg.), Positionierung der außeruniversitären Sozialforschung* (Wien, 1999), pp.31–46.

[20] A profile of the institute dating from the beginning of 1988 contains a list of the research projects that existed alongside the finished or current 'football studies', which includes, amongst others, two studies in the preparatory stage (one on the 'problems and needs of students in secondary education' and the other on 'cultural development planning') together with two planned research papers ('art presentation and art review' and 'how do humans turn into monsters: perception and imagination in the development and reproduction of foe images').

[21] U. Lischke and H. Rögl, *Multikulturalität. Diskurs und Wirklichkeit* (Wien, 1993).

[22] I have pointed out the somewhat irritating and often erroneous translation of the German term 'Kulturwissenschaften' with 'Cultural Studies' elsewhere. Cf. Roman Horak, 'Cultural Studies in Germany revisited', *Cultural Studies* 16:6 (November, 2002), p.884. It is, however, a special and absolutely delightful irony of fate that the IFK, which in recent years has been directed by Gotthart Wunberg and effectively run by Lutz Musner, has opened itself to cultural studies. Cf. L. Musner, 'Locating culture in the US and central Europe – a transatlantic perspective on cultural studies', *Cultural Studies*, 13:4 (October, 1999) and L. Musner and Gotthart Wunberg, 'Kulturstudien heute. Eine Gebrauchsanleitung', *bmwv / IFK (Hrsg.), The Contemporary Study of Culture* (Vienna, 1999).

[23] M. Reisenleitner, 'Institutionalizing Cultural Studies in Austria: A view from afar', *Cultural Studies* 16:6 (November, 2002), pp.896-907.

[24] Cf. Josef Hochgerner in an interview with Frank Hartmann, in F. Hartmann [ed] *Forums Sozialforschung (publ.), Positionierung der außeruniversitären Sozialforschung*, pp.9–16; *Standort und Perspektiven der außeruniversitären Sozialforschung*, (Vienna, 1993).

[25] Cf. www.univie.ac.at/IG-LektorInnen/ig.html (as of 30 November, 2003).

[26] Cf. www.culturalstudies.at (as of 20 November, 2003).

[27] European Science Foundation, ARCH (Assessing Austrian Research in Contemporary History), 'Evaluation Report', (10 July, 2003), p.84.

[28] Anne and Marine Rambach, *Les intellos précaires* (Paris: Fayard, 2001).

[29] Anton Pelinka, 'Die Politik der ÖVP-FPÖ-Koalition und die neoliberale Deregulierung', Paper from the conference 'Stress durch Politik', (16 March, 2001, Vienna).

[30] Chantal Mouffe, 'Why the left needs a political adversary not a moral enemy' (www.eicp.net/diskurs/d04/text/chantalmouffe02.htm [as of 10 December, 2003]).

[31] Günter Hefler, 'Wie es uns geht […] Kommentar zu Anne und Marine Rambach – *Les intellos précaires*. Paris 2001: Fayard', *Grundrisse. Zeitschrift für linke theorie und debatte* 5 (www.unet.univie.ac.at/~a9709070/5es_uns_geht.htm [as of 19 December, 2003]).

Roman Horak is Head of Sociology of Art and Cultural Sociology at the Institute of Aesthetics and Cultural Studies/Art Pedagogy, University of Applied Arts, Vienna. He was a founding member and co-director (1985–1992) of the '*Institut fuer Kulturstudien*' (IKUS) in Vienna. From October 1988 to March 1989 he was Honorary Visiting Fellow at the Department of Sociology, University of Leicester, and since 1998 he has been a member of the Editorial Board of *Cultural Studies*. He has published a number of books, most recently *Die Praxis der Cultural Studies* (Vienna, 2002).

parallax, 2004, vol. 10, no. 2, 100–116

Whose Accountability? Governmentality and the Auditing of Universities

Cris Shore and Susan Wright

Introduction: 'Coercive Accountability' and the Rise of Audit Culture[1]

One of the most interesting aspects of the transformation that has been occurring in universities in the United Kingdom and elsewhere over the past decade and a half has been the extraordinary proliferation of new managerial discourses of 'accountability' and 'excellence'. What we seem to be witnessing throughout the university sector, as in numerous other domains of life, are the curious effects of what anthropologists have termed 'audit culture',[2] and in particular, a form of 'coercive accountability' that can be explicitly linked to the spread of a new form of managerialism based on neoliberal techniques of governance.[3] The key features of this new regime of governance include, *inter alia*, a fixation with the measurement, quantification and 'benchmarking' of seemingly all aspects of university life; the invention of a plethora of new 'performance indicators' (not to mention the creation of a whole new vocabulary to enable the new auditor-experts to assess and rank 'quality' and 'excellence') and an explosion of new league tables to render commensurable hitherto unimaginable phenomena. Thus, we now have national league tables that rank everything from hospital deaths, police responses, academic output and benefit fraud, to court occupancy, beach cleaning, cervical cancers and primary school test results. All of these areas and more must now be scrutinized, quantified, statistically ranked and 'rendered visible' either to the consumer or, as in most cases, to the anonymous gaze of the State and its bureaucratic machinery.

Michael Power's book *The Audit Explosion*[4] was one of the first systematic attempts to document the way in which the incessant drive toward ever more detailed and intrusive forms of accountability and control through audits is re-shaping the modern work place. As he noted a decade ago, 'there is a real sense in which 1990s Britain has become an "audit society"'[5]: that is, a society in which people have come to think of themselves as 'auditees', and one where it is no longer possible to think of accountability without elaborately detailed policing mechanisms. The main argument for audits is that they bring greater transparency, efficiency and quality and therefore 'trust'. They also facilitate surveillance and regulation of the workforce, rendering it both more productive and more 'accountable' to management. However, as Onora O'Neill[6] and Michael Power have shown, audits often have the opposite effect, obscuring what is actually happening in the workplace, fuelling suspicion and mistrust, undermining professional ethics and generating a host of unforeseen problems.

parallax
ISSN 1353-4645 print/ISSN 1460-700X online © 2004 Taylor & Francis Ltd
http://www.tandf.co.uk/journals
DOI: 10.1080/1353464042000208558

The aim of this paper is to try to make theoretical sense, from an anthropological perspective, of the way in which these new managerial regimes of audit and accountability are reshaping public institutions – in this case the university – and beyond this, to reflect on the implications of these changes for understanding contemporary forms of governance and power in advanced industrial societies. However, to situate our discussion in a wider and more empirical context, we begin with three stories that, in their different ways, illustrate the problem of accountability that this paper seeks to grapple with.

The Audit Society: Three Contemporary Tales of Accountability

In June 2002 it was announced that Birmingham University's internationally renowned Department of Sociology and Cultural Studies had been earmarked for closure by the end of the following month. This came as a shock, not only to staff within that Department, but also to the wider academic community in Britain and beyond. Why had Birmingham University's new Vice Chancellor and Management Team decided to close one of their most successful and internationally prestigious departments – widely regarded (at least in the wider academic community) as one of the jewels in its crown? Certainly not for financial reasons: the Department was economically buoyant with 250 undergraduates and 50 postgraduate research students and with the anticipated arrival that autumn of a further thirty, mostly high fee-paying, overseas research students (something that most university departments can only dream of). Nor for its poor reputation: the department had a proud heritage and enjoyed enormous international prestige as the founder of modern Cultural Studies. Nor too because of poor teaching records or low staff morale: the department had just achieved a perfect 24 in its last Teaching Quality Assessment and its staff were primarily young and highly motivated teachers and scholars.[7] The official answer was because of the department's 'performance' in the 2001 Research Assessment Exercise (RAE). The new management team, in its *University Plan*, had decreed that a '3a research rating' was unacceptable; hence, members of the department were 'invited' to take voluntary severance or else face the threat of compulsory redundancy.

Our second story concerns National Health Service waiting list figures.[8] In March 2003, an enquiry by the Audit Commission revealed widespread misreporting of waiting list figures in no less than 22 of Britain's 41 NHS Trusts, including several cases of 'deliberate and systematic fiddling' of the figures by hospital managers themselves. In these so-called 'waiting list scams', patients who were close to the six-month limit were either reclassified so they appeared on different lists, or else simply excluded from the list altogether if they had been waiting too long.[9] The requirement to collect such statistics was designed precisely to press hospitals to meet government targets of reduced waiting times. Perversely, the effect was to make many patients wait much longer than the maximum permitted time for treatment. Despite making headline news and being denounced by the chief executive of the NHS as 'reprehensible and inexcusable', the expressions of surprise and moral indignation were widely seen as disingenuous. If hospitals are paid per 'medical incident', and then punished for failing to meet government performance targets, it is hardly surprising that managers massage the figures. Indeed, the system would seem to encourage such behaviour.

In May 2003 further evidence of the close correlation between performance targets and cheating emerged: news broke that Ministers had warned hospital managers that those whose hospitals failed to meet targets for waiting times in Accident and Emergency Departments would be out of a job. Hospital managers had also been informed that the judgement whether they had met their targets (which in turn would determine their star rating and their funding for the next year) would be based on the performance of their A&E departments during one week in March. The target was for 90 percent of casualty patients to be discharged, admitted or transferred to another hospital within four hours. Many hospitals were normally 10 percent below this target. Hospital managers poured 'hundreds of thousands of pounds' into their casualty departments 'drafting in extra doctors, nurses and radiographers in the week they were assessed. Some went as far as cancelling dozens of operations to free up beds for casualty patients'.[10] Most hospitals hit this target, but returned to normal levels of spending and of performance the following week. A government spokesperson called it 'human nature'[11] and did not criticize hospital managers for working the system, and saving their jobs, in this way. Indeed, it was in government's interest to be able to proclaim that hospitals were meeting their targets and that their policies were succeeding. Two of the hospitals that had cancelled their operations were among the 'best performers' and had been earmarked for designation as 'Foundation Hospitals' under the latest 'flagship' policy that the Blair government had pushed through the Commons, despite major opposition within the Labour Party.

Our third story, also widely reported in the British media in March 2003, concerned a former head teacher from a primary school in Maidstone, Kent, who was jailed for three months for forging hundreds of his pupils' 'Stage 2 SATS tests'. These national assessment tests for all children at different stages in their primary education were partly designed to identify successful or failing schools. The results are published as league tables in order for parents to select, on the basis of these performance indicators, the best school for their children. Poor results will lead to loss of pupils and a loss of core funding, and may trigger a downward spiral towards 'special measures', or even closure. The court had heard that this head teacher had felt under pressure from the publication of league tables and financial difficulties at the school.[12] However, for the judge, his crime was 'so serious' that an immediate custodial sentence was required. In his summation, the judge argued that: 'If others were to act in this fashion the whole system would be immediately and utterly destroyed, and that cannot be allowed to happen'. Despite these punitive sanctions and stern proclamations, the pressure that SATs tests have placed on schools to improve their performance and 'ratings' has led other head teachers to act in exactly this fashion.[13]

'Accountability' as Political Technology: A Duplicitous Concept

Three separate tales that in their own way chronicle life in contemporary Britain, but are they linked, and is there a deeper message or meaning to be gleaned from these stories? In one sense they do share a common theme: all three reflect symptoms of what might be termed the modern 'cult of accountability'. But what is interesting about these stories – aside from the evidence of regulatory failure – is that they highlight the way in which audit and accountability are being used to drive forward a neoliberal ideological agenda and inculcate the values of enterprise culture within the public sector – even if this sometimes leads to 'creative accountancy' in order to meet performance targets. What we have witnessed over the past decade has been the development (or 'migration') of the idea of audit, from a set of practices linked to financial regulation and control to a more general tool of management that is being used in all walks of life, from local government and the health service to education, the arts and the media. From a practice once confined to the annual ordering of business accounts, audit has spread to the measurement and ordering of culture itself, and in the process, has given birth to a distinctive kind of 'audit culture'. Nowhere is this more evident – or its influence more deleterious – than in the British university system.

At the same time, the concept of 'accountability' has been given a new twist and meaning within this system of new public management. As a concept, accountability has many positive associations with terms like 'openness and transparency', 'responsibility' and 'democracy' that no reasonable person could oppose. However, there are many different forms and styles of accountability, some of which are not as democratic or benign as the term might imply. The key question is not simply 'who is being made accountable to whom?' but rather, 'what are the socio-cultural and political implications of the technologies that are being used to hold people to account?'

Within British higher education accountability has become the watchword for a new system of corporate management based on performance indicators and target setting. In short, audit has become the principle mechanism for securing accountability. However, in the past, other forms of accountability prevailed. Ivar Bleiklie[14] argues that universities in the early nineteenth century were conceived primarily as autonomous cultural institutions whose role was to provide a social critique, independent of the State. In the United Kingdom this principle was given clearest expression in the 1919 Haldane reforms. Confronted with a serious financial crisis after the First World War, universities accepted government funding via the University Grants Committee, a quasi-autonomous body that disbursed government money to the universities with the minimum of 'guidance'.[15] However, in order to guarantee their immunity from direct government interference, universities were granted Royal Charters, which made them autonomous organizations in law. Formally at least, the old universities are still defined as independent organizations in their own right, and not as parts of government or the public sector (however, in practice, as we argue below, the rise of the new public management regime has eroded, and continues to erode, that tradition).

Within this 'autonomous' model the professoriate was responsible for overseeing academic standards and professional competence. In the early American version, disciplinary departments performed this role. It was the role of professors and heads of department to maintain institutional autonomy and protect universities from outside interference. The line of accountability was internally hierarchical, but university teachers were not expected to answer directly to government. Nor was it considered appropriate for governments to intervene in the design of the curriculum, the examining process, or the recruitment of staff. In Britain, the principle of institutional autonomy was also bound up with the concept of intellectual freedom and the idea that universities should be arbiters of their own academic standards.

According to Bleiklie, this early model of accountability was overlaid by another layer of expectations about the function of universities as public agencies for the preparation of candidates for top civil-service posts and the learned professions. This role involved the State, as the politically and financially responsible authority, in attempts to manage universities through legislation and budgetary policy. The line of accountability here contradicted the model of universities as autonomous cultural institutions. Yet a third layer of expectations has arisen with the post-1980s model of the university as a corporate enterprise. Here the university is conceived as a producer of mass education as well as research services and 'knowledge transfer' in what governments today call the competitive, knowledge-based global economy. In this managerial model, the university is accountable, through its senior management teams, to government and must meet its specific policy goals and standards of provision.

Rather than replacing each other, Bleiklie suggests that these three models now overlay each other. Each suggests a different organizational architecture and each has different lines of accountability that are not always compatible. Furthermore, even within the current corporate managerial model there is a tension between decentralization of responsibility and decision making to Schools and Departments, and strong, centralized leadership. The problem today, as Bleiklie suggests, is that these different layers of expectations have gradually been piled upon one another. Each of these roles – as autonomous cultural institutions, public agencies and market-oriented corporate enterprises – requires different standards of loyalty, quality and efficiency. He concludes: 'It is hard to imagine how all of these expectations might be achieved simultaneously'.[16] The resulting internal contradictions provide plentiful scope for allocating blame when things go wrong. It is also one of the justifications for ever-more intrusive forms of audit and accounting.

How Accountability is Re-shaping Universities

Of Bleiklie's three discourses, it is clearly the 'university as corporate enterprise in the knowledge industry' that dominates today. This is changing the university's role as public agency and weakening its classical definition as a cultural institution. 'Efficiency' and a 'consumer orientation' have become the core values with personnel management as the central means through which to realize these goals. In Britain it was the 1985 Jarratt report that set the agenda for reforming universities into corporate enterprises in a competitive market. That report focused particularly on the need for tighter management structures and processes.[17] Thereafter, Vice Chancellors were re-baptized as 'Chief Executives', departments became 'cost centres', and university administrators became 'managers'. These semantic shifts were highly indicative of the ethos and ideology driving the university reform process.

In many respects, Bleiklie's historiography of university discourses on accountability parallels Bill Readings's provocative critique of the university in the contemporary era of transnationalism. Like Bleiklie, Readings also identifies three historical phases (or ideas) in the history of the function of the modern university: the Kantian idea of 'reason', the Humboldtian idea of 'culture' and the techno-bureaucratic notion of 'excellence'.[18] As Readings notes, the Enlightenment idea of the liberal university of culture – based on the idea of the pursuit of knowledge as an end in itself – is being supplanted by a conception of the university as a transnational bureaucratic corporation, although this transition between old and new narratives is not necessarily sequential or absolute. As he puts it, the 'new hero in the story of the university' is no longer the professor who is both scholar and teacher but the administrator whose task is to re-organize the institution in terms of a generalized logic of 'accountability' in which the university must pursue 'excellence' in all aspects of its functioning.[19] However, and here Readings's analysis is at its most acute,[20] 'excellence' is a pseudo-scientific index that has no content. Like the cash-nexus, it is neither true nor false and its domination carries with it no automatic political orientation or regime of truth. The modern discourse of excellence – and the 'pursuit of excellence' – is thus able to present itself as above politics or ideology. 'Its very lack of reference allows excellence to function as a principle of translatability between radically different idioms: parking services and research grants can be excellent, and their excellence is not dependent on any specific qualities or effects that they share'.[21] The discourse of excellence thus not only contrives to produce a single standard in terms of which universities can be judged externally, it also functions as the unit of value through which universities can understand themselves within the logic of corporate administration.

Another important mechanism by which universities were to be rendered more entrepreneurial and efficient in their pursuit of 'excellence' is through the introduction of measures to instil greater 'cost consciousness'. By making departments into 'cost centres' it became easier to measure staff-student ratios. Departmental income was calculated in terms of a statistical construct called 'FTEs' (or 'Full-Time Equivalents'). This financial measure was based on the fee income of a department's various categories of students. Irrespective of the actual teaching needs of mature, overseas, part-time, access, disabled and standard-entry students, it was their financial 'yield' to the university that determined the staff allocation. A ratchet principle was applied whereby additional staffing resources were only given a year *after* the student numbers had increased. As one London college principal remarked in an address to staff at the beginning of term, 'When you look at a new student, don't see an individual, see the cheque they're carrying on their head'.

A second measure for instilling cost-consciousness involved the auditing of staff research productivity. The RAE (Research Assessment Exercise) was created to measure and rank the research publications of all departments in order to construct league tables of 'excellence'. Government core funding for research was allocated to each department on the basis of its ratings. This system spawned yet another bureaucratic managerial edifice within universities to plan the RAE process, collect statistical data, monitor performance and supervise the writing of submissions. Perversely, for a system designed to promote cost-consciousness, the RAE generated unprecedented costs in terms of staff time, energy and stress.

Parallel with this drive for efficiency and economy – and to offset fears that increasing work loads on staff and rising staff-student ratios would result in falling standards – policy makers also instigated a series of measures aimed at 'quality assurance' and 'quality control'. Foremost among these was the TQA (or Teaching Quality Assessment) – another system designed to measure and rank departments. The results were then published (in the name of transparency) and transformed by newspapers into national league tables which arguably influenced student choice (and therefore departmental income) in subsequent years.

There are interesting parallels here with the rise of accounting and accountability in the nineteenth century. Accounting for the use of labour and raw materials in production processes was ostensibly aimed at enhancing efficiency and productivity. However, as Hoskin and Macve[22] have demonstrated, in the first factories where these accounting techniques were developed, they in fact yielded no improvements in either of these measures. In their words, 'accountability was not economically productive'. However, it did prove extremely effective as a mechanism for disciplining and controlling the workforce. As one of the workers in Carnegie's company remarked in 1870:

> The minutest details of cost of materials and labor in every department appeared from day to day and week to week in the accounts; and soon every man about the place was made to realize it. The men felt and often remarked that the eyes of the company were always on them through the books.[23]

In this way, workers were transformed into calculable and calculating entities. Such accounting worked to instil within workers the habits of self-discipline so that they might work upon themselves to improve their own productivity and performance. Accountability procedures in universities have similarly transformed staff into 'auditable selves'. They are ever-conscious of how they are 'performing' in relation to audit criteria: Are they creating a convincing paper trail as evidence of the quality of their teaching and student support? What evidence can they adduce that students have acquired the 'learning outcomes' projected for their courses? How can they persuade enough students to return their course evaluation questionnaires? How can they fit in these bureaucratic demands and still try and find time to prepare classes and meet students? When will they have time to read and think or should they instead be producing more visible 'outputs' for their putative research time? Moreover, the auditable self is not just reflecting on his or her own performance but comparing and competing with colleagues and other departments. No one wants to be labelled a '3a researcher' or the under-performing 'tail' at the end of the department's next RAE submission; everyone in the department needs to ensure they keep or improve their current rating in order to protect their department's income and therefore their own time for research.

As in the 19th century, under the guise of measuring performance and efficiency, these accounting instruments functioned primarily as methods for asserting managerial control over ever-larger units, and for breaking the resistance of a potentially troublesome workforce. The overriding goal behind the contemporary drive for efficiency and quality, it seems, is also to discipline and control the workforce. 'Efficiency', as Bruneau and Savage observe, 'is not an end in itself – one must ask, efficiency in aid of what goals? A central goal must be power, since without it political, social, or economic policies are unlikely to be realised'.[24] A similar argument is made by Loughlin:

> The purpose of this quality jargon is not to improve services but to locate power in the hands of those who control quality mechanisms and to deliver support for government policies.[25]

Measures for securing economy, efficiency and 'quality assurance' in the modern university arguably have little actual positive impact in improving quality,[26] but they work extremely effectively as instruments for introducing new forms of governmentality, bureaucratic rationality and management control.

The Quality Revolution: Assault of Rhetoric, Consolidation of Managerialism

Whereas Hoskin and Macve document the genesis of accountability in the universities and track its migration outward to corporations, the 'quality revolution' has been in the opposite direction; from industry to the universities. The origin of this managerial doctrine is attributed to Phillip Crosby's *Quality is Free*.[27] Crosby asserts that quality cannot rely on subjective 'professional judgement' but must be based on empirical and objective measures that can be ticked off a list and read off documents like a balance sheet. To him, 'quality is too important to be left to professionals, who always think they "know best"'.[28] As Loughlin points out, however, the advocates of 'quality management' invariably reject rigorous analysis of the meaning of the 'criteria' which supposedly provide the intellectual foundations of their 'science'.[29] Instead they brow-beat their audience with a barrage of rhetoric: 'quality', 'excellence', 'autonomy', 'empowerment', 'continuous improvement', 'enhancement', 'dynamic learning cultures', 'ownership', 'effectiveness' and 'self-actualisation'. Rather than defining these terms, those in power simply explain one of their 'criteria' in terms of another with a semantic circularity that recalls what anthropologists sometimes call a 'closed' conceptual system. The effect of this is that managers choose whichever operational definition of 'quality' suits their purpose. Whereas 'QME' (or 'quality management and enhancement') was one of the six 'aspects of provision' that academics had to pretend they understood and demonstrate they delivered in the Teaching Quality Assessment, even the chief executive of the QAA (Quality Assurance Agency) casually let slip that he too had no clear idea what quality enhancement meant.[30]

If those designing and running the audit systems can chose whichever word, or definition, from this semantic circuit suits their purpose, managers can also choose to deploy their new tools in order to discipline and control certain 'troublesome' individuals. Julie Marcus describes a system of public accountability in New South Wales, Australia, which was first designed to root out corruption among senior politicians, and high level police and public servants. But universities and the whole apparatus of publicly funded bodies also come under the legislation and its definitions of corruption are so broad that any small slip has the potential to fall within its reach. As Marcus describes it, ICAC, the New South Wales agency set up to implement the legislation, focuses on the easiest targets, the small fry. According to Marcus, what began as a 'crime prevention' body has mutated into a crime invention entity:

> It views the tiniest misdemeanour as seriously as the greatest corruption, makes small crimes into large ones and creates a network of regulatory processes that will produce the small crimes it takes so seriously.[31]

The agency has powers far greater than a court of law. It can take away academics' computers, read their email and listen to their phone calls; it removes the accused person's right to silence and requires them to respond to accusations. Universities hold over staff the threat of referring cases to this agency. Meanwhile, under their own audit procedures university managers can require information and search through records without having to notify the academics of any specific accusation against them or provide a forum in which they can respond to the case and clear their name. This process means that each administrative query has the potential to become a crime investigation or a case of alleged 'corruption'.

Marcus herself was appointed as professor of a new department, formed amid dissent, and given a remit to improve the quantity and quality of research – a situation of plentiful potential tensions. Rather than dealing with the problems created by establishing a new department with new and unwelcome goals, the university's managers allowed the finance department to follow up specious allegations and small mistakes, inflating them into a fraud and corruption investigation that, after seven years, has never been properly tested or resolved. The audit issues were so minor as to be laughable in any other circumstances. But internal auditing practices combined with the New South Wales anti-corruption legislation converts the messy details of everyday administrative life into a field of potential criminality.

One recent example of these shifts illustrates the point. In processing documents required for research travel, Marcus's very efficient office omitted to ensure that permission for Marcus to use her own car for fieldwork was obtained before the travel commenced. In the past, permission was always taken for granted and finance staff had never previously queried what was a clear case of customary practice. When reimbursement for travel expenses was requested, it was refused, leading to a process of investigation that after eighteen months, is still unresolved.[32] Such glitches, of the kind academics make frequently within the increasingly complex web of regulation, are easily corrected and are of little significance to good governance. Other lecturers at the university who made such 'errors' received a phone call from the finance office to establish the situation and correct the paperwork. In Marcus's case, such a minor administrative error became one of the bases of a fraud investigation. When no fraud was found, they conducted 'fishing expeditions' looking for even more cleverly concealed corruption in all aspects of Marcus's research and handling of the department. She describes the process as 'brutalising', 'fantastical and unreal'. Marcus argues that this search for micro-evils is targeted at specific people, making them dangerous to know, but has a wider effect, isolating the victim, frightening other staff and fragmenting opposition.

Accountability of Managers?

This case raises questions about the accountability of managers, and the way in which the concept of accountability is employed. The need to guarantee the formal independence of auditors also means that their actions are not fully supervised, let alone transparent or fully costed. As Marcus comments:

> In addition to terrorising the academic community and dividing it against itself, the use of false accusation, constant scrutiny, innuendo, fishing expeditions aimed at finding something and anything to complain about, no matter how small – all serve to divert attention from those busy hurling thunderbolts at others [...] The apostles of transparency and propriety go unscrutinised and uncontrolled.[33]

Similarly, in England the line of 'accountability' that has been strengthened by the measures of quality and excellence in teaching and research is invariably 'upward', from lecturers to management. However, management itself, as Evans points out,[34] is the one area of higher education that has not been reformed or made accountable, either upwards or downwards. Management seems to occupy an exalted, unaccountable position in universities today.

> [I]n case after case, those entrusted with responsibility under the subordinate legislation of an institution fail to follow its requirements without repercussion for themselves. They break the domestic laws and the rules of natural justice. They dismiss members of staff without due process. They discipline students without telling them that they have a right to know of accusations against them and to be given an opportunity to defend themselves. Perhaps the member of staff or the student succeeds in litigation against the university, but the individual or individuals guilty of the breach of the internal regulations are unlikely to be called to account.[35]

The lack of accountability of Vice Chancellors and senior management for the ways they manage their staff and other resources is compounded by the problem of weak and ineffective governing councils. These are largely unelected bodies. Typically, their members receive little or no professional training in the duties entrusted to them as governors or how to fulfil their responsibilities. Most are selected for their putative experience of running large and complex organizations, for their standing in the world, and for their strong-minded independence. However, many are in fact intimidated by the principal of the institution, who is often present at meetings. The enquiry into mismanagement by the former principal of the Southampton Institute revealed the 'surprising degree' to which governors could feel themselves intimidated, and the 'depressing' fact that they were unable to blow the whistle.[36] The governing council can also be simply by-passed and not informed of major decisions taken by the senior management team, as seems to have been the case at Birmingham. The University Plan, stating that RAE 3 rated units would be reviewed 'with a view to restructure' went through Council on 26 June 2002 without a whisper about closure or staff redundancies.[37] Yet the week before staff in the Department of Cultural Studies and Sociology had received letters informing them of the closure of the department and 'inviting' them to take voluntary severance. In other instances, some members of a governing body may even owe their selection to their close personal ties to the Principal or Vice Chancellor, and may act in sympathy or collusion with him or her, rather than responding to requests from staff and students for thorough enquiries into the management of the organization. Elected representatives of university lecturers are usually only a small and marginal minority on these governing bodies.

Students – usually through their union – have only a token representation. Thus, the majority of members who are legally responsible for the governance of the university do not have a working knowledge of how it runs.

University accountability appears to be a one-way street. Poor performance in teaching or research is now easy to expose. What constitutes poor quality administration, by contrast, is seldom defined – either in practice or in law.

> League tables of maladministrative incidents, misconducts in public office, mismanagements, cases taken to the employment tribunal, complaints and appeals from students, breaches of domestic legislation would tell the world a great deal that universities would rather it did not know.[38]

This accountability blind spot is what enables management to value their own activities so highly, and to reward them accordingly. As Simon Hoggart writes in his review of Robert Protherough and John Pick's *Managing Britannia*:

> Because management is seen as a good in itself, managers feel free to spread it everywhere. Frequently the methods it involves don't work, which means that more managers are required to force it to work. Managers set wages, and since they rate management very highly, managers get the fattest pay packages. This draws more people into management and away from actually doing whatever their organisation is supposed to do.[39]

If universities are to be remodelled as corporations, the private sector does not set them a good example. Irrespective of the performance of their listed companies, company boards are notorious for awarding their chief executives bloated pay increases and bonuses, despite the outcry of their shareholders, to whom they are formally accountable. Sir Philip Watts, Chairman of Shell, for example, missed his financial targets, presided over a 27 percent slump in the share price of Shell in 2002–03 and has plans to lay off 4,000 staff. Despite this record of performance, he has been rewarded with a 55 percent pay rise bringing his salary to £1.79 million. He has also received a £1.167 million increase in the value of his pension while the company pension schemes for his workers have been closed on the grounds that they are now too expensive to run.[40] Senior managers even have a vested interest in failure when, for example, HSBC offers its new Director an annual 'bonus' of $4 million irrespective of performance and, if he is sacked, agrees to pay him £37m including free shares and free health and dental care for himself and his wife for the rest of their lives.[41]

While the remuneration of university 'chief executives' is still not on a par with that of private corporations, there is a similar discrepancy between their pay levels and those of their workers. In the 2003 pay round, lecturers in England received pay increases of 3.5 percent, while for vice chancellors the average was 6.1 percent, and thirty three of them accepted an increase of between 10 and 27 percent.[42] In the 1970s, 'university staff' was a category that applied to both lecturers and Vice Chancellors, all of whom were seen as embodying the university. Today there is a wide gulf separating 'staff' from 'management'. Whereas administrators *supported* academic staff in the past, now academic staff *work for* management. Managers have become the apparatchiks or Nomenclature of higher education: a 'New Class' that appears increasingly detached – both economically and socially – from those lower down the managerial food chain.

'Public' Accountability?

According to Bleiklie's earliest model of university accountability (above) it was the responsibility of academics to provide an independent critique of society and culture and provoke public debate. Many academics cling to this view but the universities' 'public' role is now rarely referred to in policy debates in Britain. Charles Clarke, the Secretary of State for Education, recently claimed that universities' main responsibility is to help transform society to meet the needs of the economy – a far cry from critiquing the effects of capitalism's latest global phase on society and culture. In Clarke's instrumental view, subjects such as philosophy and history that have traditionally provided this kind of critique do not deserve government funding and should be only minimally retained as an 'ornament' to society.[43] In Australia, the New South Wales anti-corruption agency described by Marcus[44] makes much reference to universities' 'public' role, but with a new twist to its meaning. To this agency, academics are a dangerous anomaly and a high corruption risk because they are not recruited and managed like the rest of the state funded sector. Civil servants are recruited to the service as a whole, they advance their careers by moving from one department to another, and they are socialized into identifying with the government's notions of public duty and public interest. Academics, although state funded, do not identify with these notions. They see themselves as employees of a specific university with its own autonomous procedures, and prize their freedom and independent judgement. This makes them, according to the agency, more of a corruption risk than public servants. Marcus argues that under the guise of 'public' and 'financial' accountability to the government of the day, this agency is adding audit procedures to the forces which act against university autonomy and academic independence, as the vestiges of professional values which predated the transformation of universities into corporations. Against this view Marcus marshals the old argument that universities are not accountable to the government but to the public in general and that it is the public duty of academics to maintain academic freedom and intellectual independence.

In England there is no similar contest over the meaning of the 'public' accountability of universities. Instead, the White Paper argues that universities are to be accountable to their 'primary stakeholders', the students.[45] Students are to be made to contribute to the costs of their education[46] and they join the government as the principal funders of universities. According to the corporate model, universities are delivering a service (education) to their customers (students) to whom they owe accountability. Universities must now respect their consumers' rights. They must collect and respond to student feedback on the quality of university provision. They must provide applicants with 'accessible information' about the quality of their courses and of the 'student experience' in order for students to become 'intelligent and efficient customers'. Students' choices about which service to buy will then become the mechanism to 'drive up quality' in universities. Like 'quality', however, the criteria for defining and measuring the 'student experience' are, as yet, undeveloped. The information collected from each cohort of students about their experience will no doubt be collated, published and used to construct further league tables to competitively rank universities according to yet another set of bureaucratic criteria.

Part of the rationale behind this move is to change the way students are positioned within the discourse and management of higher education. Traditionally, as Anwar Tlili argues, students 'have been positioned as the object of higher education policies and discourses; always absent from decision-making processes, simply standing at the receiving end of Higher Education management'.[47] Now students are to be empowered 'through recognising and codifying their rights that derive from their definition as customers and investors […] to whom universities, the providers, are accountable'. However, there is a striking absence of detail about how students will be empowered to use their voice to 'drive up quality' and hold universities to account. Indeed, as a mobile and transient population, it is particularly difficult for students to have a sustained input into the policy process and hold universities to account. Course monitoring and feedback on departmental programmes are no doubt beneficial to universities in their quest to improve teaching provision, but that is not the only level at which the gaze of accountability is needed. These feedback processes also gather information about deficiencies in provision, administration and governance at the university level. Rarely, if ever, are there adequate mechanisms for the relevant officers to collect this information, let alone act upon it. In one such 'staff-student monitoring committee' meeting chaired by one of the authors, in which students raised problems about top-up fees, library hours, exam scheduling, student records and centralized timetabling of classes, the problem was summed up by a mature 'adult' student: 'It seems as if all the problems we raise that can't be dealt with at departmental level fall into a big black hole'.

Significantly, the White Paper makes a point of defining students as 'adults' in the sense that they must pay their own way in funding their education, and it states that surveys will ensure the student voice is heard, but it does not offer any effective democratic machinery for students to be a presence in decision making forums and voice their views themselves. In contrast, in Scotland the funding council has made a more serious attempt to include students in the membership of committees throughout the Universities' decision making systems, unless there are good reasons for their exclusion. In England, university staff have a justifiable fear that government and management teams will appropriate the 'student voice' and use information about 'the student experience' to further their own policy priorities. In other words, far from treating students as 'adults', the absence of any effective democratic machinery for students to voice their own experience and call the organization to account means that it is government itself that will speak for them, as if in *loco parentis*.

Conclusion: Accountability and Blame Culture

We began this paper with three examples of the ways in which pressure to meet and conform to new performance indicators and standards of efficiency are affecting institutional behaviour. In all three cases, the aim was to use performance indicators and league tables to identify and reward successful universities, hospitals and schools and put pressure on those deemed to be underperforming. But the way the audit system was applied to each sector was different. Hospital managers manipulated their figures and played the system, and government turned a blind eye. Government was committed to pushing through its next stage of hospital reform and needed 'evidence' that its policies to get hospitals to improve their performance were succeeding. Head teachers were under the same pressure as hospital managers to meet performance indicators, but when they worked the system or cheated, they were picked out as individuals and severely punished.

If the system can be applied differentially between sectors, institutions can also use the audit system to target particular individuals (as in Marcus's case) or single departments. Birmingham University's Department of Cultural Studies and Sociology was highly successful in terms of most of the standard criteria for evaluating success. Indeed months later, whilst the students were continuing to struggle against their department's closure,[48] and Birmingham AUT called for an independent inquiry into management's handling of the matter, the disbanded staff team found their provision of Sociology ranked in first place and of Cultural Studies ranked in second place in the Education Guardian's national league tables. Nationally, media and communication and communications and cultural studies were among those 'newer' disciplines that as a whole received low research scores and the Funding Council allocated extra development funds to all these departments to help improve their research. These arguments cut no ice with Birmingham's senior management who used the low RAE score as the 'reason' to quickly close the department and make staff redundant (although they kept the undergraduate students and their income). Within a year, the University advertized three posts in cultural studies and eight in sociology and accepted the funding councils' development money.[49] Senior managers seem to think that in a couple of years the international fuss will have died down and forgotten, so new generations of students will be attracted to the old, famous brand name and the income from the new department will again become buoyant. Still no one can fathom a justifiable reason for closing the department. Maybe the Department had a reputation within the University for being troublesome. Maybe it was because a new Vice Chancellor and his new management team wanted to assert their control over the institution. The previous senior management team had intervened and changed the RAE entry at a very late stage, removing a quarter of the department from the submission, against the Head of Department's protest that this would lead to a lower score.[50] The responsible Pro-Vice Chancellor promised one of the staff affected that he would take responsibility if his strategy was unsuccessful but staff could find no way to hold senior management to account. In the wake of the 2001 RAE, the new senior management team's strategy was for all departments to return at least 90% of their staff in the next RAE with at least 85% of staff working in 5 or 5* rated units.[51] An example needed to be made to press this point home and to show staff that the senior management 'meant business'. Senior management demonstrated to the rest of the University that they had the power to close one of the University's most famous departments, ride out the storm of protests from the UK and around the world, and treat the letters and petitions from their 'primary stakeholders', students and their parents, and even from their MPs 'with utter contempt'.[52]

The Birmingham example illustrates the main point of this article: namely that the so-called 'quality revolution' with its rhetoric of 'empowerment' and 'accountability' is geared less to enhancing quality itself than to strengthening managerial control over the workforce. In each of these examples, 'accountability' is confused with accountancy, while 'self evaluation' is reduced to a matter of the institution's ability to demonstrate to external inspectors that it has internal systems of quality control.[53] The question is 'whose accountability?' While the discourse of quality management promotes the idea that every individual is empowered with responsibility for the organization and its success, the effects of accountability are not evenly distributed. The machinery of accountability targets the lower echelons of the organization and deflects the eye of scrutiny from the higher levels, especially where, as in universities, mechanisms for professional and public accountability at the highest level are poorly developed. There may be mechanisms for financial audit, but there are seldom adequate systems for scrutinizing the performance of senior administrators and managers and making them accountable to either staff or students.

For some, no doubt, the quality revolution is a long-overdue process of rationalising and modernising public services, making them answerable to their funders and consumers, their stakeholders and the tax-payer. In this view, cost-consciousness, efficiency and value for money carry positive connotations as they are meant, ultimately, to benefit the public and the consumer. However, for those inside the organization, the quality revolution is associated with a culture of blame. Whereas the rhetoric of quality enhancement emphasizes each individual's contributing equally to the success of the organization, when things go wrong, blame is disproportionately targeted at the lower orders. As the examples of Vice Chancellors and Chief Executives discussed in this essay show, not all stakeholders in an organization are 'equal' when it comes to salary increases, not all are subject to equal levels of scrutiny, and not all take the consequences for when things go wrong.

Notes

[1] We would like to thank Peter Kilroy and the editors of *parallax* for their detailed comments and suggestions on an earlier draft of this paper.

[2] Marilyn Strathern, 'Introduction: new accountabilities' in Marilyn Srathern [ed], *Audit Cultures: Anthropological Studies in Accountability, Ethics and the Academy* (EASA Series, London: Routledge, 2000).

[3] Cris Shore and Susan Wright, 'Audit culture and anthropology: neo-liberalism in British higher education', *Journal of the Royal Anthropological Institute*, 5:4 (1999), pp.557-575. Cris Shore and Susan Wright, 'Coercive accountability: the rise of audit culture in higher education', in Strathern [ed], *Audit Cultures*.

[4] Michael Power, *The Audit Explosion* (London: Demos, 1994).

[5] Power, *The Audit Explosion*, p.1.

[6] Onora O'Neill, 'A question of trust', *BBC Reith Lectures*, Radio 4 (3 April–1 May, 2002).

[7] Rebecca Boden and Debbie Epstein, 'It all adds up to a pretty Brum do', *Times Higher Education Supplement*, 1556 (20 September, 2002), p.14.

[8] Jeremy Laurence, 'Waiting list figures fixed in bid to hit NHS targets', *The Daily Telegraph*, 5 (March, 2003), p.2.

[9] BBC News Online, 'Q & A: Waiting list fiddles' (Tuesday, 4 March, 2003) (http://news.bbc.co.uk/2/hi/health/2819111.stm).

[10] Jo Revill, 'Hospitals faking cuts in casualty wait times', *The Observer* (11 May, 2003), p.1.

[11] Jo Revill, 'Hospitals faking cuts in casualty wait times', p.1.

[12] BBC News at Ten (7 March, 2003).

[13] In May 2003 a head teacher from Reading was reprimanded by the General Teaching Council for allowing pupils to cheat in their science and maths SATs. Two days earlier, head teachers had discussed boycotting national primary and secondary tests and demanded the abolition of

exams for seven year-olds, *The Guardian* (7 May, 2003).

[14] Ivar Bleiklie, 'Justifying the evaluative state: new public management ideals in higher education', *European Journal of Education*, 33:3 (1998), pp.299–316.

[15] Berdahl, 'Co-ordinating structures: the UGC and US state co-ordinating agencies' in Michael Shattock and Burton R. Clark [eds], *The Structure and Governance of Higher Education* (Guildford, Surrey: Society for Research into Higher Education, 1983), pp.83–84.

[16] Bleiklie, 'Justifying the evaluative state', p.310.

[17] Michael Allen, *The Goals of Universities* (Buckingham: Open University Press and SRHE), p.125.

[18] Bill Readings, *The University in Ruins* (Cambridge Mass.: Harvard University Press), p.14.

[19] Readings, *The University in Ruins*, p.8.

[20] While much of our analysis and that of Bleiklie's concurs with Readings's thesis, we would caution against his definition of the modern university as 'posthistorical'. We also find his attempt to explain the transformation of the modern university in terms of the demise of the nation state problematic and unconvincing.

[21] Readings, *The University in Ruins*, p.24.

[22] Keith Hoskin and Richard Macve, 'The genesis of accountability: the West Point connections', *Accounting, Organisations and Society*, 13:1 (1988), pp.37–73.

[23] Chandler 1977:267–8, quoted in Hoskin and Macve, 'The genesis of accountability', p.67.

[24] William Bruneau and Donald Savage, *Counting Out the Scholars: The Case Against Performance Indicators in Higher Education* (Toronto: James Lorimer and Co., 2002), p.11.

[25] Michael Loughlin, 'Assurances, effectiveness, ownership, empowerment, autonomy, dynamic learning curves [...] a continuum of quality awareness, self-actualisation and enhancement [...] whatever that means', *Times Higher Education Supplement* (22 March, 2002).

[26] A study to test the belief that Ofsted inspections would raise academic standards concluded that in 1,933 of the most common type of comprehensive secondary schools over 6 years 'Ofsted inspection had no positive effect on examination achievement. If anything it made it worse'. I. Shaw, D. P. Newton, M. Aitken and R. Darnell, 'Do Ofsted inspections of secondary schools make a difference to secondary school results?', *British Educational Research Journal*, 29:1 (2003), pp.60–75.

[27] Philip B. Crosby, *Quality Is Free: The Art of Making Quality Certain* (New York: Mentor Books, 1979).

[28] Crosby quoted in Loughlin, 'Assurances'.

[29] Loughlin, 'Assurances'.

[30] In his *Times Higher Education Supplement* article, Peter Williams explained that 'Quality Assurance' is not the opposite of 'Quality Enhancement [...] whatever that word means', *Times Higher Education Supplement*, (11 January, 2002), cited in Loughlin, 'Assurances'.

[31] Julie Marcus, 'Criminalizing academics: ICAC and audit culture in the universities', (unpublished paper, 2003).

[32] The investigation into Marcus's travel expenses discovered that one receipt for accommodation did not show an 'Australian Business Number' (required for tax purposes). Rather than contacting the business to ask for the number, the university refused to pay the entire expenses claim for approximately 1500 Australian dollars. This 'error' could have been corrected very easily, but the absence of the 'ABN' was used as a reason to question the validity of the whole claim for reimbursement of research expenses.

[33] Marcus, 'Criminalizing academics'.

[34] G. R. Evans, 'Quality Assessment and the Administration and Management of Universities: Ways and Means', *Higher Education Review*, 32:2 (2000), pp.3–16.

[35] Evans, 'Quality Assessment and the Administration and Management of Universities', p.11.

[36] Minutes of Evidence to the PAC Report on the Southampton Institute, quoted by Evans 2002:9.

[37] Frank Webster, 'Death of a department', *The Guardian* (15 August, 2002).

[38] Evans, 'Quality Assessment and the Administration and Management of Universities', p.13.

[39] Simon Hoggart, 'A plague of managers spreads destruction', *The Guardian* (March 2, 2002) (www.guardian.co.uk/comment/story/0,3604,660571,00.html).

[40] Katherine Griffiths, 'The face of corporate Britain', *The Independent* (24 April, 2003), p.1.

[41] Editorial 'Shareholders in revolt', *The Guardian* (28 April, 2003). In a first sign of revolt, shareholders of GlaxoSmithKline in an 'advisory' vote, rejected the company's plan to give its chief executive Jean-Pierre Garnier £22m if he were to lose his job. Jill Treanor, 'Rebels humiliate Glaxo over pay deal', *The Guardian Weekly* (22–28 May, 2003), p.1.

[42] Alison Goddard, 'Union fury as VCs pocket 6% pay rise', *Times Higher Education Supplement*, 7 (February, 2003), p.1.

[43] 'Clarke asks what the state should pay for. Extracts from Charles Clarke's speech at University College, Worcester on April 8', *Times Higher Education Supplement* (16 May, 2003), p.3.

[44] Marcus, 'Criminalizing academics'.

[45] *The Future of Higher Education*, (London: Department for Education and Skills, Cm 5735, 2003).

[46] The costs to a student of a BA degree (fees and living costs) are now estimated at between £16,000 and £20,000.

[47] Anwar Tlili, 'Students in the White Paper', Paper delivered to the C-SAP Conference: 'Dynamics of Change in Higher Education', (Birmingham, 3–4 April, 2003).

[48] Tony Tysome, 'Protesters play "spot the similarity" over cutbacks', *The Times Higher Education Supplement* (13 June, 2003).

[49] Birmingham AUT report on the meeting of Senate on 19 March, 2003.

[50] Webster, 'Death of a department'.

[51] University of Birmingham, *The University Plan 2002–7* (2002), para.R2.

[52] Lyn Jones MP speech to the conference 'Whose University?' held at Birmingham University, 10 May, 2003.

[53] Cf. Power, *The Audit Explosion*, p.19; Readings, *The University in Ruins*, p.32.

Cris Shore is Chair of Social Anthropology at the University of Auckland and, until May 2003, was Professor of Anthropology at Goldsmiths College, London. His current research interests lie in the field of political anthropology, particularly the anthropology of the State. Recent books include *Building Europe: The Cultural Politics of European Integration* (Routledge, 2000) and *Elite Cultures: Anthropological Perspectives* (edited with Stephen Nugent, Routledge, 2002). He is also author and co-editor (with Susan Wright) of *Anthropology of Policy: Critical Perspectives on Governance and Power* (Routledge, 1997) and several essays on the rise of 'audit culture' in higher education.

Susan Wright is professor of educational anthropology at the Danish University of Education, Copenhagen. Her recent publications have been on the reform of higher education, and especially the introduction of 'audit culture' in the UK. She is now researching university reform in Denmark. Her publications (with Cris Shore) include *Anthropology of Policy: Critical Perspectives on Governance and Power* (Routledge, 1997), 'Audit culture and anthropology' (*Journal of the Royal Anthropological Institute*, 1999) and 'Coercive accountability: the rise of audit culture in higher education', in Marilyn Strathern [ed], *Audit Cultures: Anthropological Studies in Accountability, Ethics and the Academy* (Routledge, 2000).